THE LAST ENEMY

The Last Enemy

A CHRISTIAN UNDERSTANDING OF DEATH

Richard W. Doss

HARPER & ROW, PUBLISHERS

New York
Evanston
San Francisco
London

1817

FIRST EDITION

Designed by Sidney Feinberg

Library of Congress Cataloging in Publication Data

Doss, Richard W
   The last enemy.
   Includes bibliographical references.
   1. Death. I. Title.
BT825.D697   1974   236'.1   73-18700
ISBN 0-06-061980-5

To Barbara

Contents

Preface

This book is one result of a research project begun in early 1969 under a grant given to the American Baptist Seminary of the West by the Forest Lawn Foundation. Mr. Frederick Llewellyn, Chairman of the Foundation, and a long-time supporter of higher education, suggested that the foundation would be interested in a seminary faculty member working on the theological significance of death and the funeral. I was interested in the subject, as I had discovered while pursuing graduate study that very little writing had been done on the theological understanding of death. The work was undertaken with the intention of producing two volumes: one on a theology of death and the second on a theology of the funeral.

I have written this book with the serious layman and the practicing minister in mind. In so doing I have avoided much terminology of the technical theologican. I am hopeful that the book may be of use in church school classes and study groups. In the early days of the research I was given able assistance by a friend and student, Steve Snyder. Dr. C. Adrian Heaton and the administration and faculty of the American Baptist Seminary of the West, Covina Campus have been most cooperative and helpful. Dr. Genevieve Kelly and Mrs. Helen Thomas have been especially helpful in searching for bibliographic materials. My students in three seminars on the theology of death have criticized my ideas and provided new ones for me. The Rev. Robert Huston has provided opportunities to interact with and speak to ministers. My three children, Mark, Beth, and Tim, and most important, my wife Barbara have provided help, inspiration, and support.

Introduction

Several years ago a distinguished biologist, winner of the Nobel Prize, Professor George Wald, addressed a Boston audience on the subject: "A Generation in Search of a Future." Speaking in somber tones, he listed some reasons why students and the youth culture were concerned about the future. It was an impressive list: the war in Vietnam, the compulsory draft, mammoth expenditures by the Defense Department disposing of old bombs and nerve gas, building outmoded weapons in the name of security, the stockpiling of nuclear weapons, an exploding population, and the destruction of our environment. And then Dr. Wald made this statement: "I think I know what is bothering the students. I think that what we are up against is a generation that is by no means sure that it has a future."[1]

Nor should we think it is only the youth culture that is concerned about the future. Our vocabulary grows with terms like "futurology" and "futurism." One of the most widely read books in recent years is Alvin Toffler's *Future Shock*. Sociologist Toffler coined a new term to describe the psychological responses people are making to rapid change in our society. In the next three decades vast numbers of people will experience an abrupt collision with the future, Toffler claims, and fall victim to tomorrow's most menacing malady: the disease of change. Unable to face the overwhelming pace of change, the continuous demands to adapt to novelty, many people will plunge into future shock.

Religion is contemplating the future. During the sixties a new movement in theology took shape and rapidly came to this country. Led by German scholar Jürgen Moltmann, "the theology of hope" firmly claimed that the place to start in the study of religion and theology is at the end—with eschatology, the study of last things. "There is only one real problem in Christian theology," Moltmann writes, "the problem of the future,"[2] A popular response is found in Hal Lindsay's *Late Great Planet Earth,* a book that has sold over four million copies. Using a speculative, crystal-ball approach to the future, Lindsay provides for his readers a road map into the future, a newspaper forecast of things to come.

Concern for the future by Christians is not unfounded. One need only glance at the pages of the New Testament, especially the sayings and teachings of Jesus, to discover a major emphasis given to the future. The purpose of Jesus' teaching was to announce that in him the kingdom of God had become a present, powerful reality. He stated clearly that God's kingdom had begun, but he also indicated that the kingdom would one day come in its fullness. He pointed his followers to the future. In the preaching of Jesus we find a call to hope and faith in a God who is the power and promise of the future. Jesus wants his disciples to take the future seriously and realistically.

All of this leads me to make an observation, and indeed, to state the motivation behind this book. I have carefully read and studied books that speak of the future and the meaning of Christian hope. In analyzing the concerns and elements of futuristic literature, one event is noticeably absent. Popular literature avoids it and sophisticated theological literature is strangly silent concerning it. I am speaking about the fact of death—the most important and significant event, it seems to me, in my future and the future of every man. Yet, while these writers have sought to provide a realistic statement about faith and hope, there is a conspicuous silence concerning death.

The silence is understandable. Death is not faced openly in our culture. The American attitude toward death is one of denial and repression. Death has become the new obscenity and the literature of death the new pornography. In polite society we are prudish about death, making it a taboo that is "disgusting and immoral and not to be talked about."[3] Mass media confronts us daily with the harshness of death and our attitudes about death. Yet even in an atmosphere of denial there are some encouraging signs that the taboo is being lifted and the silence broken.

Death has become a subject for vigorous study by men in academic disciplines. Universities have established centers to study and investigate the meaning of death psychologically and socially. Two new scholarly journals have been started to provide an opportunity for the publication of research on dying, terminal care, reactions to death, and recovery from loss and bereavement. A number of important studies have been conducted on the subject of suicide. Several collections of articles are now available dealing with death and religious belief. Yet interest, while growing, is still primarily limited to the borders of the academic community.

And so this is a book about death. If you are unwilling to face death and specifically your own death, you will not want to read further. But if you are willing to deal with "the last enemy" in an open way, then let's get on with it. There will be times, I'm sure, when the discussion becomes somewhat obtuse and rather obscure. I am a working theologian and obscurity unfortunately tends to be part of our territory. Yet I do want to be understood—I have no desire suddenly to bring forth my hidden agenda. The main point I want to make is extraordinarily simple, and like most simple truths it is one thing to say it and another thing to understand and feel the importance of it. Here it is: death is the one event in my life which confronts me with the question of the meaning and purpose of life and the significance of the future. If I affirm the value of life right now and hope for the future, I must do so openly and realistically in the face of death. It is the facing of death which forces me to deal with the question of ultimate meaning.

One further thing needs to be brought into the open by way of introduction. My approach to the subject is in no way unbiased. I come to the issue of death as a Christian, one who finds in Jesus Christ a way of facing and dealing with the vital issues of life. I am convinced that every Christian needs a theology of death to put life in its proper perspective. This theology is more than a system of belief or recital of dogmas held by the Church. We need a theology that helps us make sense out of life, intellectually and emotionally. We need a theology that is responsive to the culture and the world in which we live. I believe a theology of death must speak of more than faith for the future, although it must certainly do that. It must deal with the demands and risks of faith right now.

In a conviction that our culture and environment has had tremendous impact on the ways we think and feel, the discussion begins with an exploration of the ways death is handled in American society. It then moves to the development of a theological style, attempting to show how we move toward an understanding of theology which meets our own emotional and intellectual needs. The remainder of the book attempts to elaborate the basic elements of a theology of death. Certain important topics are mentioned in only the briefest way; this has been necessary in order to deal with the central issue. I have found that being a Christian has helped me face the reality of death, find meaning in both life and death, evaluate the power of death honestly and realistically. I sincerely hope this book will help you do the same.

THE LAST ENEMY

CHAPTER 1

Death and the
American Life-Style

The American way of death is a carefully manipulated style utilizing tools of silence, denial, and avoidance. Death is no longer a part of God's purposes or an inevitable mystery of life. Death has become a logistical problem for the systems analysts who deal with it—doctors, funeral directors, clergymen, lawyers—even a few sociologists who describe the entire process. The American way of life is systematically eliminating death—a kind of planned obsolescence. British historian Arnold Toynbee, a perceptive commentator on the American scene, claims that death is an unmentionable word in our vocabulary because "if the fact of death were once admitted to be a reality even in the United States, then it would also have to be admitted that the United States is not the earthly paradise that it is deemed to be (and this is one of the crucial articles of faith in 'the American way of life')."[1]

Why the conspiracy of silence? What has happened in our culture to cause this repression and denial of death?

The avoidance of death is distinctly a twentieth-century phenomenon in American life. In secure, quiet rural America, death was faced openly as an inevitable consequence of man's mortality. Although never looked upon as a friend, death was spoken of freely with the dying and with children alike. In a not unfamiliar scene, small children and friends gathered at the bedside of an elderly grandfather. Death occurred in a familiar environment. A religious framework explained the meaning of death as part of the will and purpose of God. Hope of life after death eased the anxiety with which one contemplated the future. Men believed that when this earthly pilgrimage was ended, they would awaken to find themselves in the presence of God.

But this framework for interpreting the meaning of life and death is gone. Many people in the Church still accept it, but it is no longer woven into the fabric of our culture. Modern American society has been cut loose from its religious moorings. The idea of finding meaning in terms of a suprasensory, otherwordly realm seems quaint and primitive to men influenced by science and technology. The modern American seeks whatever meaning there is in the here and now. Questions about my identity, value, and dignity cannot be dealt with in terms of a divine plan or purpose. We are aware that our forefathers found their hope in a future life. The mood of our time is to find our hope here and now. Postponement as an act of faith or frustration is no longer possible.

There is a clear shift from a Christian worldview to one that is post-Christian. This shift began centuries ago when men first began to take themselves seriously and consider the potentialities of being human. With the industrial revolution and the resulting technology and urbanization, the focus of man's confidence changed from the sacred to the secular, from the world to come to this world. Our culture today is dominated by this secular spirit. Secularization has brought a radical shift in the setting of human life. Men today do not look to an eternal changeless order to which we must accommodate ourselves, but to a radically changing environment to which one must adapt. Institutions, traditions, and customs are no longer seen as given by God or supernatural authority, but as cultural products which are changing, and indeed, must change. There is an increasing impatience with those who procrastinate concerning the pressing issues of justice, peace, population control, and pollution—in short, human survival. Emphasizing life right now means that people are demanding that things be done right now.

Secularization has stripped death of the structure and meaning by which it was traditionally interpreted. The secular spirit leaves death denuded, and thus we look on it as an accident or communicable disease. Robert Fulton, a sociologist who has spent much of his career studying the effects of death on our society, observes: "Death is now a temporal matter. Like cancer or syphilis, it is a private disaster that we discuss only reluctantly with our physician. . . . Death, like a noxious disease, has become a taboo subject, and as such it is both the object of much disguise and denial as well as of raucous and macabre humor."[2]

In this sense British social anthropologist Geoffrey Gorer speaks of "the pornography of death." Death is pornographic in that it is an unmentionable aspect of human experience, something dealt with only as an object of private fantasy. Unmentionable as a natural process, death is thereby isolated and left alone.[3]

The dilemma of modern secular man is that while he affirms the importance of his own autonomy and his life in the here and now, he is unable to devise a way of facing the future while experiencing the power of an authentic hope in the present. But how can anyone face the future and affirm the meaning of hope without honestly confronting the reality of death? Death is the boundary that shapes and defines my future, that limits my life and forces me to deal with my mortality and finitude. At this point secular man feels the horns of his dilemma. Death is denied, privatized, and isolated in order that finitude need not be faced. If death is a matter of medical engineering, then human finitude is not necessarily a final word. Why worry and fret about death's finality while the engineers are working on the problem? The words of philosopher William Ernest Hocking are too true: "Man is the only animal that contemplates death, and also the only animal that shows any signs of doubt of its finality."[4] And so our society attempts to push death into a corner—to camouflage death or repress it from consciousness. The unfortunate result is an unhealthy neurosis about the future and an inability to face openly the crisis experiences of life.

1. DENIAL OF DEATH

Franz Borkenau, political commentator and historian, noted that cultures can be analyzed and described by their attitudes toward death. He contended that the experience of death is a basic element shaping the course of history and is traceable to individual and communal attitudes within given cultures. He found in ancient Greek culture a death-accepting attitude. In Judaeo-Christian culture, Borkenau discovered a death-defying culture. This note of defiance is clearly sounded in the words of St. Paul: "O death, where is thy victory? O death, where is thy sting?" (I Cor. 15:55). And in modern, post-Christian culture, Borkenau finds a death-denying attitude. Denial leads to a loss of personality and individual worth and results in a quest for value in some higher unit—the state or party—an expression clearly found in fascism and communism.

Behavioral scientists agree that ours is a death-denying society. Herman Feifel, a psychologist who more than any other person has been a motivating force in researching death, claims that as an individual occurrence, it has been blurred by institutionalization and an embarrassed lack of curiosity. "In the presence of death, Western culture, by and large, has tended to run, hide, and seek refuge in group norms and actuarial statistics."[5] Researchers are agreed as to the fact of denial, but not much information is available tracing its reasons. I find three major reasons for the denial of death in our culture.

The first is psychological. The basic insight found in the writings of the founder of psychoanalysis, Sigmund Freud, postulates that every person in the unconscious mind is convinced of his own immortality. In observing his own patients, Freud discovered that denial functions as a coping mechanism enabling patients to handle their anxiety about death. Every time we attempt to contemplate our own death, Freud noted, we do so as spectators, that is, we are unable to think about or imagine our own nonbeing. However, there is danger in denial, for when death is not faced, life becomes flat and superficial like a flirtation where nothing serious happens.[6]

Following the insights of Freud, Elisabeth Kübler-Ross contends that the violence and destructiveness of modern life could be alleviated if we made an all-out effort to face our own death and the anxieties surrounding it. Denial enables us to live in the midst of massive violence, to watch the bombings of Vietnam on television, to hear the reports of highway deaths, to realize that people are dying all around me, and yet at the same time privately maintain that it will occur "to thee and to thee but not to me."[7] Dr. Ross relates the incident of one woman who was shocked and outraged over the "unfair death" of a young man killed in an automobile accident shortly after returning from Vietnam. This woman somehow believed that survival on the battlefield provided a guarantee of the young soldier's safety at home. This kind of denial promotes an unreal outlook on life and death.

Freud's psychoanalytic insight gives us a clue to the destructive function of denial. Our culture tolerates violence and war as flirtation and fascination with death. This explains why, for example, Americans accepted acceleration of involvement in Vietnam for so long before widespread protest arose, why the American public could take such a blasé attitude toward the massacres and atrocities in My Lai. "Oh, we know they did worse than that!" was an all too common response. We can bear with violence so long as it is depersonalized. So long as death only confronts me only in terms of statistics, body counts, and troop withdrawal, then it can be kept in control.

Understanding the psychological need to deny death helps explain why so many people involve themselves in groups and movements which promise immortality. The power of these ideas of immortality is their denial of death—if the soul of man is immortal, then death doesn't really matter. Death is merely a door, a moment of transition, the final liberation. This theme will be more fully developed in Chapter Five. The way people cling tenaciously to the hope of immortality indicates that more than religious need is being met—deep psychological need is being dealt with. Anxiety about death is overcome through belief in an immortal soul as the absoluteness and finality of physical death is denied.

A popular expression of the promise of immortality clearly denies the reality and finality of death. It is the technological immortality of the cryonics movement. Cryogenics is the branch of physics dealing with cold temperatures. Karl Werner, a designer of underwater structures, coined the term "cryonics" to describe the preservation of the human body through freezing. Using the slogan "Freeze-Wait-Reanimate," the Cryonics Society of America seeks to promote the hope that death can be eliminated through freezing. The problem of death is one of medical engineering, as cryonics advocates see it; thus the promise of technological revival provides men with the hope of a solution to the cause of death. Unmoved by the skepticism of scientists and physicians, cryonics movement leaders contend that freezing at least offers man a chance of survival, "a chance of debatable magnitude, but nevertheless some chance."[8] In my mind this is the worst kind of exploitation, preying upon those willing to clutch at any means of overcoming their anxiety about the finality of death. Furthermore, it removes any chance of dignity for the dying in a last minute frantic effort to freeze the body for a possible future reanimation. It is a costly and unwarranted form of denial.

A second reason why American society is death-denying is cultural.[9] We live in a culture where the "American life-style" is promulgated with evangelistic zeal. Who is the happy, successful American? Answer this question by looking at the advertising in popular magazines. Notice the emphasis on youthfulness, vitality, and productivity. The worth of a man is measured by what he can produce. Doing is the criterion for being. Little wonder that Americans have such difficulty handling leisure time or retirement! I have a friend who spends every vacation in a remote wilderness spot, chopping wood and pumping water, and every year he returns from his vacation exhausted but released from the guilt he felt about taking time off work. Vitality is the foundation of this lifestyle. We place a high premium on the aggressive, vigorous individual filled with boundless energy. Little wonder that death, the direct opposite of vital life, is denied.

And what about the "youth cult" in America? Think and act young—eat the right kind of cereal, "Mama," and your daughter's seventeen-year-old boy friend will mistakenly throw you into the swimming pool. We face a continual assault from the media concerning sex and youth as a way to sell the product. We have been so persuaded that sex and youth are tied together that when a mangy old Lion named "Frasier" sires a brood of offspring, he immediately becomes a national hero. "Frasier for President" imprinted on the front of a sweatshirt—what more could any lion want? My point is that the American advertising industry has led us to believe in our potential for wholeness only as thinking and acting young. Popular magazines, especially those aimed at a female audience, offer assurance that despite the fact a woman is over thirty, there can still be hope for finding value and meaning in life. As one might expect, the profit motive is no small part of the induced youth mania. A prepackaged Madison Avenue "youth cult" has helped to create a completely new industry, a "health industry," complete with gyms, beauty spas, exercise clubs, and health food stores—the modern counterpart to the fountain of youth. Death is not the last enemy to a youth-oriented American culture. It is an enemy to be fought and conquered right now.

A third reason that helps to explain our death-denying culture is religious and theological. Religion has been a major force in shaping the ideas and life-style of the American people. Our forefathers came to this country with a clearly defined view of man and the world. From the Puritan settlement of New England to nineteenth-century life on the western frontier, a theological framework supported and interpreted man's place in society and his relationship with nature and God. Men believed and felt that God had a purpose for life, and more, that every man could know and understand God's plan. Death was one element within this religious framework and thus could be dealt with openly and treated as a natural part of life. Burial of the dead was carried out with religious rites which gave expression to this view of God's purposes for man. Burial rites supported the needs of the community to affirm not only the life of the one who died, but the life of the community as well. God, man, and the community were integrally tied together in the funeral service.

We will attempt to explain in some detail in the next chapter the theological framework through which death was interpreted. The twentieth century has seen a virtual abolition of the traditional Christian framework with no new proposal to take its place. Secularization has separated modern man from older understandings of man and society, and in so doing has separated death from the means by which it had been explained for so many years. As a result, death has been isolated and denuded. With no meaningful framework for understanding death, our culture has adopted a style of denial and avoidance.

Perhaps it is even more enlightening to examine the intricate and sophisticated methods we have devised to disguise death. One is to deny death completely. Advocates of this approach actually claim that death is unreal. According to Mary Baker Eddy, death is an error of mortal mind. This official doctrine of Christian Science has worked its way into the editorial policy of *The Christian Science Monitor* where the word "death" is never printed. A more pragmatic version of this method merely eliminates the word "death" from a working vocabulary, a practice common to the funeral and insurance industries. Numerous stories of famous people, such as William Randolph Hearst, tell of those who supposedly would not permit the word *death* to be spoken in their presence.

Denial may also be accomplished by toning down the harshness of death. A massive cultural conspiracy is at work in creating a "new image" for death. We attempt to reshape our understanding of death by the language we use, particularly imaginative euphemisms we have invented to soften the reality of death. Consider what takes place when a person dies. If he dies in a hospital (and the odds are he will) it will be announced that the patient "expired" and the attending physician will sign a "vital statistics form." No longer a "patient," the person enters a new state as a "loved one." The "remains" of the "loved one" are removed to the mortuary where the family arranges "the memorial estate." After "preparation" the "loved one" is placed in the "slumber room" (sometimes called the "reposing room"). If he is a member of a church, the minister announces from the pulpit or in the bulletin that "Mr. Jones has gone home to be with the Lord" or "passed to his heavenly home." The newspaper states succinctly that "Mr. Jones, beloved father, passed away . . ." This is the accepted social practice for speaking of death. If you are so coarse as to mention in a matter-of-fact way, "Did you hear that John Jones *died* last week?" people may think you to be in poor taste or indiscreet. Use of softened language indicates a strong need to deny the harshness of death.

A third method utilized by our death-denying culture is far more subtle. Professor Robert Neale suggests that we deny death by our preoccupation with it. This, according to Dr. Neale, is our way of denying the personal dimension of death.[10] Preoccupation of our culture with death is evidenced by motion pictures which have performed well at the box office in recent years. The most popular films have been those in which violent death is portrayed to the minutest detail. Several years ago on a late-night television show, author Mickey Spillane commented casually that sex and violence provided the key to his money-making novels.

Anthropologist Geoffrey Gorer's idea of death as pornographic, previously referred to, may sound strange for we have associated pornography primarily with sex. Pornographic literature refers to material designed to excite and stimulate a person sexually. But what pornography in fact accomplishes is the denial of the personal dimension of sexuality by objectifying and depersonalizing it. The human body is made an object of sexual desire apart from personal commitment and involvement. Pornography meets the needs of the one who wants the cheap thrill, while remaining uninvolved in the deeper meanings of sexuality. This dynamic helps us to understand the pornography of death. When death is portrayed apart from normal human emotions which surround it, as in the violence of films and television, it is dehumanized and depersonalized. We may respond in shock or dismay, but we are not helped to deal with the personal meaning of death. Violent acts happen to others not to me. The pornography of death enables us to project our finitude and mortality upon others without coming to grips with it ourselves.

Death, like sex, is depersonalized and sensationalized as a way of avoiding its reality in human life. We may be as prudish about death as about sex, seeing it as disgusting, immoral, and not to be talked about. Yet, since there is a need to come to terms with death, the result is perversion. We deny by means of morbid preoccupation with bizarre fantasies.[11]

2. SEPARATION OF DEATH FROM LIFE

Secularization has had another significant effect on the way our society deals with death. Death has become an institutional matter. Rarely does a person die in his own home with family and friends. Institutions now care for the individual in the final stages of living —retirement center, convalescent home, hospital—and the funeral industry in death. The result of this institutional development is the separation of death from life. We now have a generation which has been permitted by institutional structures to avoid personal contact with death.

I am in no way suggesting that we attempt somehow to reconstruct the simpler, rural way of life of the eighteenth and nineteenth centuries. But we do need to be aware of the structures of modern life and how they help or hinder us in dealing with the central experiences of being human. For example, radical changes have come about in the patterns of family life in American society. Fragmented due to mobility, the family is affected by new experiments in marriage and communal living. It is now rare to have young and old living together. The aging move to retirement communities where they find friendship, new activities, a sense of independence, and security. The advantages of these new relationships are obvious, but one disadvantage has been frequently overlooked; persons in their final years of life are separated from the rest of society, and as they are, so is the reality of death.

Life and death are also separated in the institutions of medicine. (The modern medical center carefully distinguishes between the living and the dying.) The status of patient all too often means the loss of integrity and personal identity. Modern medical care, utilizing techniques and hardware of medical technology, isolates the individual from a community of loving, caring persons. Anyone who has been rushed by ambulance in the middle of the night to a medical center—taken to the emergency room, examined and diagnosed, immersed in a strange environment of sights and sounds —understands the feelings of loneliness and isolation the medical institution provokes. The larger the hospital the more depersonalized the individual becomes. The art of medicine is lost in the new world of medical science and technology.

The medical institution provokes a unique crisis for the dying. The terminal patient is given the best treatment modern medicine can provide, but personal and human needs are frequently abandoned. Isolated on a special wing or floor, left alone by nurses and doctors, the dying face fears of loneliness and loss of identity and meaning. Too frequently the so-called fight for life by hospital personnel—the busy preoccupation with pulse, heart rate, electrocardiogram, and pulmonary functions—is a way of avoiding the human needs of the dying. Modern medicine must learn to look beyond the physical, and hospitals must provide staff and resources to deal with the whole man—his psychological and spiritual as well as his physical needs.

Separation of life from death is vividly experienced when one enters the world created by the modern funeral industry. Leaders in the funeral establishments view death pragmatically. Dealing with death is a business of profit as well as of service; the funeral industry has learned that in a society where death is avoided and disguised it is better business to emphasize life rather than death. Critics of the funeral industry Ruth Harmer and Jessica Mitford believe the motives of funeral leaders are primarily for profit and usually tend toward exploitation. Mitford contends that the funeral industry manipulates both the individual mourner as well as society at large through firm control of funeral practices and the manufacturing of new customs disguised as traditional practices.[12] Although not all critics of the funeral are as severe as Mitford, there is widespread dissatisfaction with rising costs.

A more severe problem to my mind is the mood of avoidance and unreality provoked by the funeral. Paul Irion observes that a number of avoidance mechanisms have been created in the last few decades.[13] The contemporary funeral is often characterized by an emotional superficiality that avoids the psychological needs of sorrow and grief. The American style of keeping emotions in control is supported by the funeral chapel and tremulant chords on the electronic organ. Death is an emotional experience and our style of facing death needs to be supportive to a realistic handling of this fact.

Further manifestation of the separation of death from life may be seen in the attempt of the funeral to create an illusion of life. Death is disguised by the use of embalming to restore natural color, cosmetic preparation, caskets with innerspring mattresses, and burial vaults designed to last "an eternity." The use of funeral establishments tends to move our dealing with death into the realm of the supraordinary. Most people whisper in a funeral home. Attending his grandfather's funeral, my ten-year-old son exclaimed in forthright honesty and in full voice, "Why is everybody whispering? No one's asleep!"

Few survivors are prepared to deal with the emotions and decisions involved in the funeral process. The matter of arrangements is often overwhelming: selection of a funeral establishment; buying a grave site; selecting clothing for the deceased; deciding on a casket, marker, grave liner and flowers; setting time of visitation and funeral service; contacting relatives and friends; handling personal matters of insurance and estate. And the mixed emotions of anger and frustration, loss and emptiness, the normal manifestations of grief. How can we deal with death realistically in the strange world of the funeral?

Many people today do not want to face the decisions or the emotions surrounding death, and there is a growing mood of "let's get it over with quickly!" Alvin Toffler helps us to understand the response of these people. He notes that oversimplification is one way of responding to rapid change, of keeping things simple and uncomplicated. Death frequently strikes like an electrical overload and we turn to simplification as a technique for coping with the stress brought on. A new observable pattern of the funeral is the private service or no service at all. Increasing numbers of people want their ashes scattered at sea or from the air. A group called the "Flying Funeral Directors of America" has been formed to handle requests for this kind of disposal. Again, the implicit danger in all of this is to use simplicity as a mechanism of avoidance, to refuse to deal with the reality of death and thereby inhibit the grieving process.

Grief, an important, normal response to death, is essentially a deprivation experience manifesting itself physically and emotionally. The grieving person may experience a variety of symptoms: appetite loss, a feeling of tightness in the throat; shortness of breath, the need to sigh, and an empty feeling in the stomach. Frequently anger and guilt are part of emotional response to grief. The grieving person fantasizes about numerous things and circumstances that might have been different. There is guilt about words spoken or actions undone. And there may also be anger such as that expressed by the young wife and mother who said, "He had no right to do this to me." We must deal with death in ways which lend realistic support to the grieving process. Learning to face death honestly in a culture where death is isolated can be a significant starting point.

3. A NEW DEFINITION OF DEATH

We have indicated how secularization has brought about a death-denying culture. Another significant result of secularization is the impact of technology. The relentless progress of technology, as Arnold Toynbee speaks of it, has revolutionized our understanding of life and death. Technology comes to us as the "know-how" of applied science turning dreams into realities. What was science fiction to a previous generation is today common experience. Surgical transplants, synthetic parts, devices such as blood-pressure sensors, heart-lung and kidney machines, hormone regulation, and genetic engineering are but a few of the changes brought about through technology.

Consider the fact of increased life expectancy. At the turn of this century the average life expectancy was forty-seven, while today it is seventy-two. The development of new drugs, antibiotics, nutritional improvements, better sanitation, insect control, agricultural developments—all have contributed to a dramatic reduction of the death rate. During the last one hundred years, life expectancy in industrialized countries has doubled. New drugs now control once fatal diseases, prolonging the lives of the dying. Resuscitation methods return the dead to life. Machines and organ transplants add years to a person's life where death was once inevitable.

All these changes have brought about the need for a new definition of death.[14] In the past, before the invention and use of technological devices, death was defined simply as the cessation of the vital life signs. When a person's heart stopped beating and breathing ceased, he was considered dead. The physician used means available to him—observation of breathing, listening to and checking heartbeat—to determine the presence of life. Legal statutes reflected this medical approach to the determination of death based on vital signs. Black's Law Dictionary provided the classic legal definition: "The cessation of life; the ceasing to exist; defined by physicians as a total stoppage of the circulation of the blood and a cessation of the animal and vital functions consequent thereon, such as respiration, pulsation, etc." Modern medical technology has created the need for a new definition of death to replace the older, simpler approach.

The crisis of definition took focus with the development and use of the heart-lung machine. The machine was so effective it kept a person "alive," that is, with vital signs functioning, long after hope for recovery was abandoned. Doctors were then confronted with an ethical question: Is it an act of mercy or murder to turn off the machine? The issue of "pulling the plug" is only one facet of the crisis of definition. The fact that a person artificially sustained by a machine is a potential donor of kidneys or heart forced doctors to decide when death occurred. Dr. Barnard faced this dilemma and defined "certain death" as a total lack of nerve reflexes, respiration, and heart activity. The scientific basis of this definition has been questioned because it failed to to deal specifically with the activity of the brain. The question became: Can life exist without a functioning brain?

A widely publicized report in the attempt to find a new definition of death was published in the *Journal of the American Medical Association,* giving results of a study conducted by the Harvard Medical School under the leadership of Dr. Henry K. Beecher. The Beecher report expressed the view that death must be defined in terms of a "permanently nonfunctioning brain"—a condition determined by a series of tests including an EEG, a check of responses to external stimuli, the ability of the patient to breathe spontaneously, and a test of the central nervous system. The report recommended that these tests be repeated after twenty-four hours. The question of definition is thus being determined by tests certifying that death has occurred.

Within the medical profession there is general agreement that the concept of a moment of death is merely a necessary fiction. A patient faces the perilous prospect of being declared dead merely because he is a potential organ or tissue donor. A decision concerning the moment of death must be made, and because of the ethical sensitivity of the Harvard committee, it was recommended that a declaration of death be made by physicians who are not involved in a later effort to transplant organs or tissue. Two potential dangers must be avoided: one is to hasten the moment of death for purposes of organ donation; the other is to allow the patient to linger as an "unburied corpse" sustained by machines. The dignity and value of human life must be visible as a judgment on these two possibilities.

What happens to the patient in the midst of a technological maze? Does the patient have any rights concerning his treatment, particularly concerning his own death?[15] An overwhelming majority of physicians feel that a patient should not be told if the prognosis is terminal. Yet literature indicates that a large majority of patients want to know about the seriousness of their condition. And what about the matter of treatment? Physicians have tended to act autonomously with an attitude of "doctor knows best," depriving the patient of any responsible decision concerning the treatment program. Even the issue concerning the right to end one's life needs to be considered. This is not euthanasia—the merciful ending of someone else's life—but the issue of whether a patient has the right to allow his own life to terminate, specifically through the suspension of treatment. We cannot avoid ethical and moral questions if we want to affirm the dignity and worth of life.

4. THE PERSONAL DIMENSION

An underlying assumption in the comments made thus far has been that all of us are shaped, molded, and influenced by the cultural patterns of American society. The death-denying culture in which we live has a powerful influence on our deepest feelings. If we are to be realistic and honest about our attitudes toward death, we must be willing to move against the stream of prevailing cultural opinion. Disguise and silence only make it more difficult to consider deeply the meaning of our own finitude and mortality. Death is a reality for each of us. All checks indicate that the mortality rate is still 100 percent. Yet I must honestly admit, I still find myself grasping for ways of hiding or denying death's reality. I walk into the room of a dying friend and find myself strangely uneasy about his frank and open way of talking about his own dying. I find myself wondering if I will have the same kind of honesty in dealing with my own dying.

Why is dealing with death so difficult? Why do we avoid makink a will, putting our affairs in order, making arrangements for our own funeral? Those who have worked with dying patients stress the importance of facing one's own feelings about death and dying. Physicians, psychologists, nurses, social workers, morticians, and ministers all need to contemplate deeply their own mortality and their feelings about death. Death is not merely for "thee and for thee"—it is for me. To deny my death is to deny my humanity, for death is one of the inevitable factors defining what is means to be human. The deficiency and the destructiveness of the American way of death is a rejection of our humanity. I refuse to allow a culture to deny and diffuse the meaning of my death lest it do the same to my life.

A Theological Style
for Interpreting Death

Does the word "theology" trouble you? It both troubles and sets off unfortunate memories in the minds of many people. It reminds ministers and priests of the remote and esoteric discussions that took place in the classrooms of their theological seminaries. It reminds laymen of sermons they have suffered through filled with high-sounding phrases separated from their personal problems and the issues of the everyday world. Too frequently theology has been an academic game, a "head trip" for those who know the rules and the language. Several years ago, a prominent theologian gave a lengthy address on a theological problem, and during the question period was asked what difference, if any, this problem would make for people in the Church. His response clearly illustrated the dismay many people have with academic theology: "Frankly," he answered, "I hadn't even thought about it."

But while we may want to reject this academic attitude, we need not reject theology. After all, the word "theology" means "talk about God," and there is a good deal of such talk going on. But why talk about God? What kinds of problems and situations give rise to God-talk? Perhaps you saw the motion picture *The Summer of '42,* a film portraying the struggle of three teenage boys with their sexuality and identity as human beings. The film confronts us with a number of questions: Who am I? What is the meaning of life? What is love? What is death? All these "ultimate" or "boundary" questions call for a theological response.

The fundamental assumption of theology must be that it is a response to real life and the problems and questions every human being faces. Theology, if it is to be concerned with life, must respond to issues raised by pain, suffering, despair, anxiety, loneliness, injustice, helplessness, and death. Talk about God does not take place in a vacuum but must include relationships vital to human experience—with nature, with other persons, and with God. This theology, which we may call relational, assumes that persons are primary, and that therefore what matters most to persons is of ultimate importance. Here we have a fundamental reason for dealing with death, since death is vitally important to each of us.

A theology of death becomes necessary if we want to listen and respond to the basic problems of human existence. In a sense, death calls the whole theological enterprise into question. Death forces us to examine the claim of Christian faith that in Jesus Christ a God of unconditional love offers new life and hope. Death forces us to face our claims that life can have meaning right now. And death also raises problems concerning the future, questions about a possible life after death and a final fulfillment of the goals and values experienced in this life. A theology of death must provide adequate response to these issues.

There are a number of ways to aproach theology, and one of the problems we must face is which approach to take. Every theologian has a point of view, and it is terribly important to distinguish between "the perspective that informs a systematic theology and the detailed analysis of theological doctrines."[1] The perspective I take affects everything I do; it influences the way I ask questions and the way I shape answers; it permeates every level of thought from simple statements to an overall interpretation. Too often, however, the matter of perspective operates as a kind of "hidden agenda," so that the reader is told what the Bible teaches or what the Church confesses, as if these were not influenced by the writer's own point of view. I do not want to be deceitful or subtle at this point. I have an ax to grind, a theological perspective, a point of view which I affirm strongly. My perspective grows out of my personal commitment of faith.

I find it helpful to distinguish between a personal affirmation of faith and the theological convictions and formulations which emerge from and grow out of that faith. This represents, in John Hick's words, two movements of faith: faith *in* Christ and faith *from* Christ.[2] I call myself a Christian because I have made an affirmation of faith in Christ. I believe in him as Lord and Savior. Through faith in Christ I find a way of looking at reality as a whole, at the world, at human relationships, and, perhaps most important, at the nature and purpose of God. Jesus Christ is the starting point of faith. For me this is a constant and unchanging declaration. In my conviction, Jesus Christ changed the entire course of human history; this conviction began with the experience of his changing my personal history. This personal commitment shapes my theological perspective.

The second movement of faith, faith *from* Christ, is the other side of my theological perspective. While faith *in* Christ is a primary affirmation that does not change, faith *from* Christ and the theological formulations and convictions which emerge from this movement of faith can and must change. Theological formulation is an attempt to communicate the meaning of Christian faith using the language and cultural patterns of a given age. Thus theology must utilize and function with the conceptions and spirit of a given culture. For this reason theology is a dynamic task. We must constantly reexamine and reconstruct our understandings of the Christian faith. Many people are made anxious and frustrated by the continuous changes in theology. Yet if we are to communicate the meaning of Christian faith to people in our age, change is to be expected. Recognition of the two movements of faith can help us. Our primary affirmation remains the same: "Jesus Christ is the same yesterday and today and forever" (Heb. 13:8). But our theological formulations constantly are restructured as we seek to discover new and fresh ways to communicate a dynamic faith.

This approach to theology demands a theological style open

and supportive to a dynamic view of Christian life and faith. I prefer the term *style* rather than *system* or *method,* because for me it is open-ended. Style has to do with the overall mood of a theology, whereas system tends to refer to the methodology and criteria by which it operates. I am increasingly convinced that we gravitate toward a theological style much the same way we develop a life-style. There are people who inherit a theological style; that is, they grow up in a specific religious tradition, accept it for themselves, and operate within it. For example, I have many friends who have grown up in a conservative religious tradition. Their basic life-style tends to be conservative. Their views of Christan faith, society, politics, and economics differ little from the views of their parents. They did not rebel against the tradition that has nurtured them. In a very real sense their life-style as well as their theological style are accepted as their personal heritage.

Increasingly, however, in our mobile society, people are forced to discover a personally meaningful way of understanding the Christian faith. People who accept the reality of changing life-styles also accept the fact that their views of God and the gospel are being restructured. But what shapes a theological style? For man in the Middle Ages it was his view of reality and the fact that he saw himself as a part of a great chain of being. But what about men in this decade of the twentieth century? We may call ourselves Christian, that is, we may have made a primary affirmation of faith in Christ, but we must then move on to discover a way of shaping our theological formulations which is basically integrative with the rest of our experience. Few people are able to separate their theological convictions from the emotional needs which give rise to them. The individual who needs assurance and certainly will develop a way of theology based on absolute authority as the source of truth. In this way intellectual and emotional assurance are bound together. Our theological style is a total perspective from which no element in our experience can be excluded and is a fairly accurate mirror of our basic attitude toward life.

Our specific task is to find a way of understanding and coping with the reality of death. My assumption is that the basic vitality and inner strength of a theology will be demonstrated by the way it deals with this subject. Death calls into question our claims concerning the love of God, the meaning of life, and the unexplained suffering and evil in our world. Although they may be more precise, familiar theological labels will be avoided in this discussion. Instead I will attempt to identify three theological styles and the response each makes to the reality of death.[3] Each style is identified in a broad way by the psychological need it represents.

1. NEED FOR ABSOLUTE CERTAINTY

In an era of virtually instantaneous change it should come as no surprise to discover a growing number of people searching for a way of doing theology that emphasizes permanence and certainty. Certainty is derived from a locus of authority, that is, from having a place where absolute truth is understood. Roman Catholics find this locus of authority in the Church, specifically in the office of the pope, while Protestants find it in the Bible, especially in the belief in an inerrant Bible. Because I can speak more accurately and from personal experience of the Protestant manifestation of this mood, I will limit the discussion in this way.

A variety of theological labels have been used to describe this side of the theological spectrum: orthodox, conservative, evangelical, and fundamentalist, to name the best known. The labels do represent variations within this theological style, but the common commitment and unifying factor is the assertion that the Bible alone is the absolute source of religious truth. The Bible is the inspired Word of God and is without error in the whole and in the part. Thus the primary task of the theologian is to discover what the Bible teaches on any given issue. One writer puts it this way:

Despite all that is being said and has been said to the contrary, the doctrine of inspiration is of the utmost significance and importance. If the Bible is not infallible, then we can be sure of nothing. The other doctrines of Christianity will then one by one go by the board. The fortunes of Christianity stand or fall with an infallible Bible. Attempts to evade this conclusion can only lead to self-deception.[4]

The basis and the source of absolute certainty, an inerrant Bible, is guaranteed because inspired by God, who cannot and will not give to man that which is contrary to fact. To question the truth of Scripture is to question the very nature of God himself. "If the revelation of God is not free from error, the message of Christianity must ever remain in doubt."[5]

With the basis of theological certainty firmly intact, those who deal with death from this perspective extract a framework from the Bible for understanding death. Well known within the Christian church because it has served as the traditional structure of Christian theology, this framework has influenced much of the development of Christian doctrine. A portrayal of the drama of salvation, it includes a view of history as well as an understanding of man and his relationship to the world. First given a full-blown description in the teaching of Augustine, this structure became the official theology of the medieval Church, was taken over by the Protestant reformers, found further explication in the creeds of the seventeenth century, and has come into the theology of the twentieth century as the traditional or orthodox point of view.

The portrayal of the drama of salvation goes something like this. A sovereign God created everything other than himself out of nothing. He first created a world of spiritual beings, the most beautiful of whom was Lucifer, the angel of light. But Lucifer, or Satan as we now know him, revolted against God and was cast out of heaven with those angels who joined in revolt with him. The fallen angels eventually came to this earth where Satan now reigns as "the god of this world." The first human beings, Adam and Eve, were created by God to live in perfect fellowship with him. Living as immortal beings in the Garden of Eden, the first pair were tempted by Satan and disobeyed God, sinning against him. As a result of the Fall, Adam and Eve were cast out of the Garden and suffered the consequences of their sin which included hard work, suffering in childbearing, disease, and physical death. The Fall of Adam was a fall to mortality. Yet even then God made plans for the redemption of man, a plan that was accomplished when Jesus atoned for the sin of Adam and the sins of all men on the cross of

Calvary. Individuals who place their faith in Jesus Christ will be saved and will receive the gift of eternal life, while those who do not believe will be banished into eternal hell to suffer the consequences of their sin.

Now I want to be very clear. This framework has served the Christian church for nearly fifteen centuries as a means of presenting the gospel. But it is not the gospel, just as no theological perspective controls the gospel. For Christians who equate this theological framework with the gospel itself, the abolition of one means destruction of the other. But if we distinguish between a primary affirmation of faith and a theological formulation, we see that the traditional framework is merely a formulation, even though one revered. My contention is that this traditional framework is no longer adequate to present either the gospel or the meaning of death to people in our secular age. To many people today, the story of angels being cast out of heaven or a first human pair being excluded from a primeval garden seems quaint and fanciful. The thought of a human being who could have lived forever but lost his immortality by eating a piece of fruit seems incredible. And the idea that the sin of Adam became the cause of death for all men is morally reprehensible. Informed by preachers that accepting the truth of the Bible and the Christian faith means accepting this framework, many who long for a relevant and mature faith turn away in dismay and incredulity.

At the heart of this viewpoint is a negative outlook on life and the world. This world is an evil place and our life in it essentially sinful. As Christians we are but strangers and pilgrims in an evil world. For the Christian, to die means only to leave a world of sin and sorrow, pain and disappointment, and to enter a world of blessedness and happiness. Our real hope is in a life and world to come. Protestant reformer John Calvin stresses the inherent otherworldliness of this theology when he writes, "In comparison with the immortality to come, let us despise this life and long to renounce it."[6] Revivalists of the nineteenth century sang, "This world is not my home, I'm just a passin' through." A strong advocate expresses the idea this way:

Heaven is our home. Life in this world is only the preparatory school, the staging ground, as it were, to get us ready for the much greater life that lies ahead. God does not want us to become satisfied with life in this world. To that end He sends an appropriate amount of sorrow, suffering and disappointment to each of His children, in order that their anticipation of and appreciation for the heavenly life may be the greater.[7]

Death, within this theological perspective, is the punishment and penalty of sin. When Adam disobeyed the command of God, he transformed his loyalty from God to the devil. There was no alternative but to execute the penalty of death on Adam and all who came after. Surely this is what the Apostle Paul meant when he wrote to the Church in Rome: "Therefore as sin came into the world through one man and death through sin, and so death spread to all men because all men sinned" (Rom. 5:12). But not only is physical death the punishment of sin. The penalty includes more than the mere dissolution of the body; death refers to every kind of punishment. It is the opposite of the reward God promises to those who trust him—the fate of those who will spend eternity in hell, the destiny of Satan, the fallen angels, and the demons. In fact, the sufferings of this life are but a foretaste of the miseries of hell. Because we are all members of a fallen, sinful race, God may execute his sovereign right to inflict death at any time he chooses. And precisely this irrationality and inequality of death should teach us the seriousness of our sin and the absolute sovereignty God maintains over our lives.

Death, the cause and the effect of sin, is therefore an unnatural event, one foreign and hostile to human life. Adam was created as a perfect creature. Augustine saw that the logic of Adam's situation was perfectly clear: if Adam had not sinned he would not have died. Writing in the *City of God,* Augustine gave this view its first clear statement: "The first men were so created, that if they had not sinned, they would not have experienced any kind of death; but that, having become sinners, they were so punished with death, that whatsoever sprang from their stock should also be punished with the same death."[8] Death was not part of God's original purpose when he created the first man. Adam sinned and fell to mortality. He was created as a being who did not have to die, but death came as an expression of divine anger—a curse that fills men with dread and fear because it is felt to be unnatural.

Physical death is the separation of the soul from the body. Man was created with a dual nature, a soul or spirit united with a body. At the moment of physical death the body begins to decompose and return to the elements, while the soul goes to be "at home with the Lord" (II Cor. 5:8). At the Resurrection our souls will be given a new Resurrection body with which we shall enjoy eternity. The Bible also speaks of spiritual death which is the separation of the soul from God. While physical death is the lot of all humanity, spiritual death will be experienced only by those who are outside of Christ. When the Bible speaks of a new birth, it refers to a spiritual rebirth. "Those who are born only once, the physical birth, die twice, a physical and a spiritual or eternal death. Those who are born twice die only once, the physical death. These latter are the Lord's redeemed."9

For the true believer, death is no terror or final disaster, but rather a portal through which we shall pass from this world to the next. Death is the day of coronation for the believer who leaves an earthly tabernacle for a heavenly abode. Yet death is never to be softened or sentimentalized. Even though not feared by the Christian, it remains a dreadful experience. But the Christian does not focus on death; rather his eye is on the life to come. "For the Christian there should be no more a problem of death than there is a problem of faded flowers or of a clouded sky. God has made this so clear in his word that there can be no grounds to question it."10

Here, then, is a way of understanding death with confidence and certainty. Our need for assurance is met through faith in this view of God's plan and purposes. The future is secure because the Bible gives us a clear picture of God's program. Throughout the centuries, countless numbers of Christian people have expressed their hope in this way, and many continue to do so today. I have no desire to destroy or undermine the faith of those who accept this framework; I have talked with enough people who advocate it to know that what I say will not change their mind. But I am concerned about gaining a hearing from those who feel uneasy with the tradition or have rejected it completely. To reject this way of understanding death and the Christian faith does not necessitate a rejection of the Christian faith. This framework is a way of doing theology, but not the only way; it is not to be equated with the gospel or with personal faith in Jesus Christ.

2. NEED FOR RATIONAL FREEDOM

If the spirit of our age is secular, the *modus operandi* is scientific and technological. Many Christians are convinced that any formulation of faith must be subjected to the probabilities and relativities of scientific method. God must be sought in terms of human experience. Faith must make sense, must find no necessity for the support of theological or ecclesiastical authorities. Traditional concepts and doctrines must be restructured in terms of natural or psychological processes. The idea of two worlds—this world and a world to come—makes little sense; no more does the idea of a God who lives in a supernatural realm, while we live here in the natural realm. If faith is to mean anything to people in a secular, scientific age, it must speak to our concerns right now, and it must speak in a language our scientifically influenced minds can understand.

There is a conscious reformulating within this theological style of traditional ideas of Christian belief and practice. God is not an abstract being above or beyond history and human experience, but the creative power and force in our midst, the ground and basis of reality and life. Creation is seen not as an attempt to describe or explain the origin of the earth but to affirm the world's goodness and worth. Hope of salvation is expressed as the desire for a quality of life here and now, not for a future heavenly existence where we walk the streets of gold. Eternal life is likewise interpreted as a possible present experience, not an existence separated from time and space after death. Heaven is awareness that God participates in our lives and knows our actions. Hell is the ugliness of life, the suffering and misery which continues despite God's presence. Judgment is the experience we all have of the passing of time and the realization that opportunities have passed that wll never come our way again. Here is a way of doing theology which sees faith not as an assent to religious authority, but as the courage to affirm the dignity and vitality of life—a faith chastened by the demands of reason and common sense.

This approach to theology places primary importance on man as a creature, a mortal and finite being. Man lives his life within the boundaries of space and time. The meanings which man finds in life are to be found in this present world. To live either in the past or in the future is to live inauthentically, to fail to deal with the possibilities of the present. We understand who we are and what it means to be human from the psychological and behavioral sciences; these disciplines inform us that our understanding of man must be holistic, that man is a unity of body, mind, and spirit, not two entities called body and soul. The idea of an eternal soul or some element in man's nature which will survive death becomes meaningless. Because man is a unity he must deal with issues which affect the whole of life, and these issues cannot be postponed to an unknown future—whether that future be conceived in this life or a life to come.

Death is simply the end of life, best likened to the last page of the book even as birth is the first. The end sets a limit on the quality—not the reality—of the book. So also the question of death. This life is all that we will know or experience; our lives are permanent and fixed and we leave after us things which give evidence to the reality of our experience. Death cannot be conceived as ultimate destruction for memories, children, and accomplishments continue after us. "Death cannot mean the destruction, or even the fading, of the book of one's life; it can mean only the fixing of its concluding page."[11]

But what about life after death? This is not a real option, say those who consistently work within this theological style. The idea of life after death is as absurd as a life before birth. Yet it is possible to advocate a kind of immortality: the recognition that we are immortal through our heirs or accomplishments or even in the mind of God. But a life after death where the experiences begun in this life continue is unthinkable. A personal existence apart from a body may not be conceived of, and the idea of an immortal soul unlimited by time and space makes little sense. The only life we live is here on this earth right now—only here will we find meaning or fulfillment. Reward is for the good I do right now and punishment will be experienced in this life or not at all. We must accept the reality of one God-given life without yearning for another where things will be better. Faith in God does not provide for second chances in another life but demands that we take our first chances seriously, recognizing that these opportunities will never pass our way again. We may strive for specific goals such as the betterment of some aspects of man's life, the cause of peace or racial justice, yet we do so fully aware that we may not see the realization of these goals in our lifetime. We must find fulfillment in the work we do right now, in the process of striving.

This theological style leaves us with several problems. One has to do with language. Traditional terminology is frequently used by advocates of this view, terms such as "heaven," "hell," "resurrection," "eternal life," "immortality." Yet these terms are radically changed from their original use and intention. Thus language becomes confusing if not in fact misleading. In my view those who find no usefulness in the traditional meanings of the language of the Bible or in the affirmations of historic Christianity should say so and then proceed to develop a language which expresses their meanings and intentions. This issue cannot be oversimplified or trivialized, for it is a serious problem for all who do theology.

Perhaps an even more serious issue for those who meet the need of rational freedom is an abandonment of biblical Christianity. One cannot read the Gospels without being confronted with the serious claim of the early Christians that God would fulfill his intentions in the future. Jesus claimed not only that the kingdom of God had become a present reality in his life and ministry, but that it would be brought to fulfillment in an age to come. Significant emphasis is given in the New Testament to ideas like "resurrection" and "eternal life"; in the context of these ideas the first Christians affirmed that what God had begun in this life, he would fulfill and bring to completion in a life to come. It is simply not possible to reject the idea of a life to come without abandoning a central aspect of the hope of early Christians.

The need to express freedom of faith and the right to try every aspect of Christian belief in the court of common sense is an important element in a theological reconstruction. Perhaps the issue is the matter of degree. I am sympathetic with those who approach theology in the rationalistic way, but I feel they have gone too far. The pendulum has swung, and the result is oversimplification of basic issues. We must not lose sight of the freedom of God in affirming the freedom of man and attempting to reduce God's activity to our present experience. Attempts to respond to the cries for relevance in the present age may result in a complete tearing up of the roots which gave strength and vitality to the Christian life and faith. I am afraid that reason and common sense have overpowered the will and need to believe.

3. NEED FOR A DYNAMIC FAITH AND AN OPEN FUTURE

There is, I believe, a middle way between the two theological styles we have thus far examined—one which does not hesitate to emphasize the strengths of the other two styles without being trapped by their weaknesses. Grounded in the need to find a dynamic faith, this middle way takes the primary affirmation of commitment to the lordship of Jesus Christ and applies a living faith to life in the modern world. This theology signifies an open future, one where God is free to realize his intentions for man and his creation. But how do we find a place to begin as we seek the center of the theological spectrum?

The selection of a starting point is itself a judgment of faith. Three main options are available to us. The first begins at a point common to each of us—human existence itself. We begin with man and his experience in the world. We explore fundamental issues regarding the meaning of being human. We discover that questions like "who am I?" and "who are you?" cause us to acknowledge the frailty and precariousness of life as the common experience of every human being. Wrestling with the basic ambiguities of life, we find that there is no human solution to the human predicament; at this point we see the need and the possibility of faith, a reaching out for something beyond our human situation. We see the need to speak of God's response to our human predicament.

A second option, proposed by those who contend that we must have a larger perspective than mere human existence, begins with a view of the world and the processes of life. We must start with reality itself, exploring the dynamic, interdependent relationships of which man is but a part. Those who begin here must attempt to resolve any conflict between a scientific view of the world and faith. In the words of Teilhard de Chardin, "the tension between science and faith should be resolved not in terms either of elimination or duality, but in terms of a synthesis."[12] We begin with a world in process, a world undergoing continuous change, and attempt to understand both the nature of man and God in light of our knowledge of the world.

Both of these options hold intellectual power and emotional vitality. Both have eloquent spokesmen who clearly define the implications of their theological way. Each option looks at death realistically and openly, providing a context in which an understanding of death is enhanced. Each starting point provides a way of overcoming conflict between science and religion in order that theology can utilize the best insights of the physical and behavioral sciences. And a major advantage of each in the "global village" of our world is that it is based on the ordinary experience of every human being. Each of us must deal with our own experiences in relation to the world in which we live. In a world where over a billion and a half people are not Christian and perhaps have never even heard of Jesus Christ, these options give us a valid place to begin. Yet I am convinced that both avoid the starting point which is inherently Christian.

A theology of death must begin with Jesus Christ. This is a

necessary implication, I believe, of our primary affirmation of faith. The basic assumption is that through faith in Jesus Christ we can discover a way of understanding both the nature and activity of God as well as the meaning of being human. Jesus Christ is at the heart of an incarnational or relational theology, providing a style for those who want a dynamic faith and an open future. Here is a way of theology grounded in the fundamental belief that God has given to man a revelation of himself in Jesus of Nazareth. We find in Jesus Christ a way of understanding God as one who takes the initiative, who reaches out to man in the precariousness of his existence and offers to him a word of love and acceptance. In Jesus we see that God is not some kind of unconcerned Eastern monarch, sitting on a throne in heaven, but that he is most fully known as the Spirit of unconditional love, a love experienced in relationship. In Jesus Christ we see how God works, not coercively but persuasively inviting them to come and follow him. Here is a God who comes to us in weakness, who participates in our struggles and our suffering, who expresses to us the depth of his divine care. In Jesus Christ we meet a God who leaves us with the terrible reality of death, but who refuses to allow it to be the final reality. We meet him who is the God of the living and not of the dead.

While this theological style makes no appeal to an absolute authority as the source of truth, it does utilize the formative resources of the Christian community: the Bible, experience, the traditions of the Church, culture, and reason. While we cannot take the time to deal with each of these resources here, it is important to acknowledge that they have each been clarified elsewhere. Certainly the primary source of theological insight is the Bible, for here we are confronted with the claims of a personal loving Creator who makes himself known to us in Jesus Christ. We take an extremely pragmatic attitude toward the Bible. It is a human document reflecting the attitudes and culture of people over a long period of time. Yet it is our primary record of the love and grace of God available to us in Jesus Christ, and through it we are confronted with the Word of God. Nowhere else do we find this message; nowhere else do we discover a view of God as unconditional love and a view of man as a partner and worker with God. The Bible may have limitations with regard to its prescientific view of the world and its primitive understanding of life, but here and only here do we find this view of God and human existence.

With Jesus Christ as a starting point and with the Bible as a primary source of theological insight, we have a significant clue as to what it means to be human. Jesus was born, lived, and died in Palestine, a part of Jewish life and culture in the first century. Gospel accounts tell us he was fully human in the same sense that we are. He was hungry, tired, angry, anxious, and fearful. When he thought about his own death he wanted to avoid it. Men who responded to the call to follow him and become disciples lived intimately with him during the three years of his ministry. While they came to know him as "the Christ, the Son of the living God" (Matt. 16:18), this in no way lessened their awareness of his essential manhood. And even as the early Christians proclaimed faith in this Jesus who was the Christ, they, too, continued to affirm his humanity. When, three centuries later, the Church put their faith in creedal form, it was said that he was "the same perfect in Godhead, the same perfect in manhood, truly God and truly man."[13]

I emphasize the humanity of Jesus because in much of the recent preaching and worship of the Church we have tended to overlook it. In our affirmation of him as Lord we have forgotten that his first followers were attracted to him as a man. What was it about the humanness of Jesus which was so unique and so attractive to others? I think that it was, quite simply, his freedom to be open and available, or to use Dietrich Bonhoeffer's well-known phrase, he was "a man for others."[14] I take this to mean that his relationships with other persons were shaped by love—by a distinct quality of love—*agape,* the unconditional, self-giving love he experienced with and received from his heavenly Father. The life and ministry of Jesus was shaped by this unique quality of love. The first Christians were convinced that they, too, could experience this love, and they bore witness to the fact that this love had changed their lives and helped them discover the meaning of being human. To be human is to be made for love. This they proclaimed to all men: Come and follow Jesus Christ, participating in the exciting discovery of what it means to be human.

In Jesus Christ we have a model of humanity. The model he provides is not in his own life-style, the product of his age and culture; it is in the motivating power of his life, the power of love, available to us through the presence and power of his Spirit. The Spirit of Christ enables us to take a new look at ourselves, to see ourselves as persons loved and accepted by God. Believing that God loves us just as we are, we have the courage to accept ourselves, or as Jesus put it, to love ourselves. Love of self which originates in a relationship with a loving Father is the source of of authentic relationships with other persons. And the fact we love others and give ourselves to them is the positive and visible demonstration of our love for God. The First Epistle of John puts it this way: "We love because he first loved us. If any one says, 'I love God,' and hates his brother, he is a liar; for he who does not love his brother whom he has seen, cannot love God whom he has not seen. And this commandment we have from him, that he who loves God should love his brother also" (I John 4:19–21).

The kind of faith which realizes the primacy of relationships fosters love of life and enjoyment of the experiences found in this world. Death comes as that event which destroys these relationships and ends these experiences—an intruder forcing its way in where it is nether wanted nor invited. Death is the destroyer of that distinctive quality of human life: the experience of life as communion, where human relationships are molded and shaped by love; this is the major source of our anxiety about death. To be anxious about death should not be interpreted as a sign of immaturity, emotional instability, or lack of faith. Only when we take life seriously, that is when we affirm the worth of life and our love for life, can death be taken seriously as the last enemy—the thief of life.

Death demands a response from each of us of openness to the future, for this implies openness to God. Dynamic faith in Jesus Christ affirms that God holds the future for us, not in a predetermined or prepackaged way, but as a call to himself, an invitation to be with him. The first Christians faced the future with confidence and assurance because their hope rested in God who was the ground and source of hope. This hope grew out of the relationships which they had experienced with God and the community of believers. It grew out of love, for it was their experience of love and its personal power that opened the future for them.

Openness to the future, then, implies openness to death, that one event which hangs in front of each of us with certainty. If we face the future anxiously and with uncertainty, we will undoubtedly face death in the same way. But if our hope is in God, the God of the living, the author of Resurrection faith, we can face the future openly and with confidence. The God who raised Jesus from the dead has overcome the power of death. With the hope that not even death can separate us from the love of God, we can be open to the future God has for us. I believe that dynamic faith can free us to face death honestly and realistically.

CHAPTER 3

Death and the Meaning of Life

Can we speak of a purpose to life or is all that which we experience ultimately meaningless? The question of life's significance brings us to the center of Christian life and faith. "Because of death," Albert Camus writes, "human existence has no meaning. All the crimes that men could commit are nothing in comparison with that fundamental crime which is death."[1] Camus is not alone in his claim that death negates any possibility of purpose in human existence. Many writers in our time contend that death stands as the final symbol of the futility of human initiative and striving. The questions they raise are not easy to answer. How can we speak of a meaningful life for the millions of Jews who were killed in Hitler's gas chambers? For a mongoloid child or a young mother who dies of cancer? If the Christian faith is to provide a basis for the claim that life is meaningful, hard questions must be faced.

What do we mean when we speak of the meaning of life? In a general way we might claim that a person has experienced meaning if he is convinced that his goals for life are being realized. The person who wants to make money may realize that objective. Each of us has values for which we strive as a matter of personal fulfillment. The value of material prosperity may become an ultimate goal. We need tangible signs that our goals are in the process of being accomplished. In a materialistic culture accepted signs of prosperity and wealth demonstrate that meaning is being experienced—a house in the suburbs, two automobiles, a boat, club memberships, a comfortable retirement plan, money in the bank. Visible signs of accomplishment validate my movement toward a final goal.

A distinction concerning the term *meaning* might be helpful here. One may claim that there are meanings *in* life without speaking of the meaning *of* life. The realization of particular values may provide a sense of meaning in what we are doing. But this does not imply that there is some kind of overall meaning. The meaning of a part may be affirmed without claiming meaning for the whole.

Meanings *in* life may be found in a variety of ways. A raise in pay validates a job. A student showing growth and progress fulfills his teacher. The realization of here-and-now values demonstrates meaning *in* life. But the meaning *of* life implies a claim for the meaning of the whole of experience, thus bringing us into the arena of faith. Christian faith makes this claim: Faith in Jesus Christ provides us with an interpretive response to the whole of reality. The Christian experience is based on personal faith in a loving Creator who is working out his purposes with his creation; from this point of view one may speak of man and history as having a meaning.

When we claim that life has meaning because of faith in Jesus Christ, we are not therefore protected from experiences in life which threaten this concept. Christian faith is not a spiritual life insurance policy against external threat or inner turmoil; there is no way of insuring ourselves against floods, earthquakes, fires, or other natural catastrophes, nor can we protect ourselves from mental illness or psychological breakdown. There is no protection or insulation against the basic contingencies of human existence. Each human being experiences a precariousness which calls the meaning of life into question. Here, then, is a basic paradox; we believe in the loving purposes of God, yet experience those things in life which seem to contradict such an affirmation. For many people, sickness, suffering, and death seem unfair or untimely. The sudden loss of a husband or child calls our faith into question.

The more we face our world and ourselves realistically, the

more aware we become of the smallness and insignificance of our lives. Dr. Rollo May contends that the central problem for modern Western man is his experience of himself as without individual significance. The person who once said, "I don't know who I am, but I can make people notice me," is now saying, "Even if I did know who I am, I couldn't make any difference as an individual anyway."[2] A new vocabulary describes the condition of persons in this age: emptiness, boredom, apathy, alienation, anomie, powerlessness, indifference. Loss of significance can be seen in the changed mood of students on the college and university campuses; if the middle and late sixties were characterized by activism, the early seventies is a time of apathy. One student put it this way: "The war is still going on, the draft has my number, the university administration doesn't listen to me—who gives a damn!" All this results in anxiety and despair. How can there be meaning if nothing really matters?

1. ANXIETY ABOUT DEATH

It is helpful and important to distinguish between fear and anxiety as attitudes toward death.[3] Fear is a common human emotion characterized by the fact of an object to be dealt with and faced; it is a response to a specific object or experience such as height or loneliness. Fear of death, the fear of extinction or annihilation, is natural. Since emotional responses to death are identifiable, they may be dealt with.

Death-related fears also concern themselves with life after death. Fear of punishment or rejection is especially common to those persons raised in a fundamentalist or traditionally Catholic orientation. Fear of eternal separation from God can make all other fears seem trivial. Related to this is fear of what happens to our body after death. Undoubtedly one of the reasons why people have difficulty making plans for the disposal of their body is the fear of its loss. We cannot even think of ourselves as being human without reference to our bodies. We share the uncertainty of Shakespeare in *Measure for Measure:*

> Ay, but to die, and go we know not where;
> To lie in cold obstruction, and to rot . . .

Anxiety is to be distinguished from fear in that it has no object —it cannot be faced in a specific way. We are experiencing anxiety if we have a vague apprehension that something terrible is going to happen—without knowing specific details. Anxiety is existential awareness of what it means to be finite, that is, awareness of death as a personal experience. If we could accept the fullest implication of being finite, we would have to accept the fact of our own death. We are anxious about nonbeing, and this anxiety is present in the whole process of living. We cannot escape it.

The source of anxiety is rooted in what it means to be a human being. Man is unique in that he has the capacity for self-consciousness or self-awareness. The manifestation of this capacity is man's ability to relate to himself. For example, I am aware of myself sitting at a desk typing. Even though I am concentrating on the task at hand, it is still possible for me to look at myself, to reflect on the process now occurring as well as think about how all of this took place. I can even fantasize about the future and imagine what kinds of responses will be made to what I am doing. The capacity for self-awareness is one aspect of what we mean theologically when we say man is made in the image of God. To think about my finitude and what this implies—the reality of eventual death— creates anxiety.

We cannot help but wonder if this anxiety is natural or whether it is an imperfection in the human race. Are we anxious because we have sinned against God and alienated ourselves from him? Do we sin because we're finite or are we finite because we sin? It seems quite clear that there is no attempt on the part of the biblical writers to join sin and finitude. Finite man is a part of God's good creation. The source of sin in the Bible is in man's freedom—not in his finiteness. Sin is the abuse of personal freedom, a conscious turning away from our dependence on God, nature, and other persons. Sin in this sense is the refusal to be self-critical. But sin is not always active resistance, it is also passive acceptance. Sin is not just the shaking of our fist toward God and others in a conscious act of alienation, it can also be seen as a rolling over and going back to sleep. This is sin manifested as sloth and lack of concern. Thus sin desensitizes us and blocks the capacity for self-criticism.

Anxiety is not sin although it can be the psychological condition which precedes sin. The relationship between the two can best be explained with an illustration. As a parent I am concerned about the future of my children. I want the "best" for them which is expectedly interpreted in terms of my values. As my children grow up and rebel against me they threaten my value structure. I may react to this threat by attempting to control them and force my values on them, or I may give them the freedom to make their own decisions about the future and shape their own values in the process. The attempt to control is an anxious response to personal threat, while the giving of freedom is an affirmation of their dignity and worth as human beings. In this sense anxiety is the precondition of sin. If I were not anxious about my children I would not attempt to control them and take away their freedom. The same thing may happen when a minority group in a society threatens the values of the majority and the majority responds with measures which control and limit the freedom of the minority.

Now we must attempt to understand the relationship between anxiety and death. Existentialist writers tell us that the two are related in a simple way. Man is anxious because he is aware that he will die. There is truth in this point of view. But our understanding of self-consciousness cannot be limited by an individualistic view of life. My self-consciousness includes the inputs from the culture in which I live and the relationships I have with other persons. What is unique about my life is that I am involved in an interdependent network of relationships. My identity is shaped by awareness that I am a man, a husband, a father, a professor, a clergyman. I have discovered who I am in these relationships which shape and structure my life; they have provided the context in which I discover what it means to love. And when I use my capacity for self-awareness to deal with the implications of my own death, I become conscious of the breaking of these relationships which mean so much to me. Death is not only the end of my finite life as an individual; it is the end of the relationships in which and through which I have sought to discover what it means to be human. Death is the end of life as I now know it, and whatever my hopes and beliefs about the future, it will end the relationships which have shaped my life. Anxiety about death emerges from my awareness of the possible end to my life as an individual and an end to those relationships which have made me a human being. This kind of anxiety is a natural part of life and is perfectly normal.

But there is a difference between normal and neurotic anxiety. Rollo May provides a clear distinction between the two.

If someone in the room shouts "Fire!" I suddenly look up, my heartbeat accelerates, my blood pressure rises so that my muscles can work more efficiently, and my senses are sharpened so that I can better perceive the blaze and choose a good way to get out. This is normal anxiety.

But if, as I move toward the door, I see that it is blocked and discover there is no other way out—a situation of "no exit"—my emotional state immediately becomes something quite different. My muscles become paralyzed, my senses are suddenly blurred, and my perception obscured. I cannot orient myself; I feel as though I am in a bad dream; I experience panic. This is neurotic anxiety.[4]

Normal anxiety is important to us as it helps us react to situations which threaten us. The anxiety which emerges when I hear the cry "Fire!" moves me to self-preservation. If my anxiety about death helps me to face life right now in a realistic and responsible way, it should be considered normal anxiety. But if it paralyzes me and keeps me from making responsible decisions, it is destructive and neurotic. This anxiety blocks awareness and impedes consciousness. Neurotic anxiety can prevent a person from dealing with the issue of meaning; to avoid the question of meaning that life is lived trivially and superficially. At this point Socrates was right: the unexamined life is not worth living.

2. EXPERIENCE OF DYING

Death is to be distinguished from dying. Those who have worked closely with terminal patients tell us that they do not fear death as much as they fear dying. The experience of dying produces a crisis in which the question of life's meaning must be dealt with in a completely new way. The dying person may not know how long is left to life, but he knows that there is not as much time as he would like. The question of meaning must now be brought to some kind of resolution.

Those who have worked closely with the dying provide important insights into the experience. We learn, first, that dying is a process including various levels or stages which must not be seen in a static or mechanistic way. Elisabeth Kübler-Ross discovered five stages in the dying process.[5] (1) The initial stage is the experience of shock and denial with a typical response of "No, not me!" Denial helps the person deal with the shocking news and mobilize defenses necessary for what is to follow. (2) The second phase is characterized by anger and resentment expressed in the words, "Why me?" As reality begins to confront the dying person a cathartic reaction occurs. Anger gushes out in many directions— toward nurses, doctors, hospital, family, friends—even God. (Many chaplains have had to face this anger as representatives of God.) (3) A third phase is a time of bargaining and negotiation. This is a time of postponement, of attempting to ward off what is now seen as inevitable. Bargaining may be with God or with the hospital staff. A person may speak of "dedicating himself to God" or donating his body or organs to medical science. (4) A fourth stage is the experience of depression and withdrawal. This is a time of preparation when the person begins to cut himself off from relationships which have been significant in life. It is a time of preparatory grief through which the person must go in order to be ready to die. (5) Finally there is the final stage of acceptance, which one cancer patient described as "the final rest before the long journey." Anger and mourning are over and, according to Dr. Ross, there is "a certain degree of quiet expectation."

A second important insight into the experience of dying centers on its fear, a complex emotional response involving a number of other apprehensions.[6] The most basic, fear of the unknown, may be likened to a child's fear of the dark. Fear of loneliness is experienced by the dying in large measure because of the physical and personal isolation of terminally ill persons—an isolation which reinforces the fear of loss of family and friends. While the breaking of relationships is a normal aspect of dying, it is not accomplished easily. The fear of loss of body must also be dealt with because our bodies are so much a part of our identity and self-awareness. Disfigurement of the body gives rise to a questioning of one's basic worth as a human being. Can we still be loved if we are unlovely or believe we are unlovely? And the fear of loss of identity, the loss of being "me," is experienced in dying. The dying process threatens the individual with total personal loss.

A third area where research helps us understand the dying process concerns long-standing myths about dying. A massive cultural lore has been developed over the years, stories which are no more reliable than old wives' tales. The phrase "death agony," common in deathbed scenes of litreature, is a myth exploded by those who have worked closely with dying patients. In point of fact, the final stage of dying is not an "agony" but is gradual and gentle.

The moment of death is often a crisis of distress for the dying person. For most, the suffering is over a while before they die. Already some of the living functions have failed and full consciousness goes early. Before the last moments of life there comes a quieter phase of surrender, the body appears to abdicate peacefully, no longer attempting to survive. Life then slips away so that few are aware of the final advent of their own death.[7]

A young mother who gained national recognition when the tape recorder on which she was keeping her thoughts on dying was stolen, said, "I think death is sort of beautiful. I've learned to love people. I'm not afraid to say, 'Hey, I love you.' "

Another myth about dying is that suffering is an ennobling experience which tends to bring out the best in people. Undoubtedly there are cases where this has happened. But clinical data point in the opposite direction. The fact is that suffering—by which is meant not only physical pain but psychic and spiritual suffering as well—is a brutalizing experience. The dying patient frequently manifests characteristics such as selfishness, impatience, rebellion, and ungratefulness. The moods of the dying person change rapidly. Such changes frequently bring disappointment and distress to the family, especially the Christian family who expect a high level of nobility and spirituality. Neither the family nor the patient should feel guilty about mixed responses, as they are a normal aspect of the dying process.

A fourth area deals with the question, "to tell or not to tell." Should the dying person know and be told about his impending death? One can find persuasive apologists for both points of view. Those who believe in telling the patient claim it is the worst kind of dishonesty and is, in fact, morally wrong not to tell the dying person. By not telling a person of the seriousness of an illness we deprive him of resources available in the dying process, especially communication with physician, minister, and friends at a time when support is needed. Those who feel that information about a terminal illness should be withheld maintain that the fear of death is unique and can have a paralyzing influence on an individual. Dr. Charles Wahl, a psychiatrist who has worked with terminally ill patients, says that he has seen patients driven to the brink of madness by well-meaning physicians who confronted them with the truth of their condition.

The most helpful response to the problem, in my judgment, is given by Elisabeth Kübler-Ross.[8] She says that the question is not "Should we tell?" but instead, *"How* do I share this knowledge with my patient?"* The way in which information is communicated will in large measure depend on the attitude of the physician toward terminal illness and death. If dealing with death is a problem for the physician, he will undoubtedly have difficulty in communicating with the patient. Dr. Ross is quite emphatic that the seriousness of an illness must be conveyed to the patient in a way which will not destroy hope. No physician should give a prognosis in terms of months or years to live. "I think it is the worst possible management of any patient, no matter how strong, to give him a concrete number of months or years."[9] The physician can listen to the patient and attempt to pick up any cues which would indicate a willingness to hear that the illness is serious. In some cases he might call on a clergyman to talk with the patient. In her experience of interviewing over 500 terminally ill patients, Dr. Ross notes that only two were unwilling or unable to hear of the seriousness of their condition.

A fifth insight concerns the positive function of denial in the dying process.[10] Denial is a psychic mechanism in the human organism which deals with perceived threats or dangers. Brought face to face with death, we deny it, block it, and turn it aside. We will not admit that is concerns us. Literature on death speaks primarily of the negative aspect of denial; however, denial can be a positive way of coping and putting up with what will eventually destroy us —a way of handling the awareness of death in a controlling way. We admit only as much information as we can handle. A vivid image for the positive value of denial may be found in the words of the seventeenth-century philosopher, La Rochefoucauld: "The human mind is as little capable to contemplate death for any length of time as the eye is able to look at the sun."

The positive value of denial is closely related to hope. Many patients have been given hope upon learning that only 90 percent of the people with the same illness they have die. They immediately see themselves in the surviving 10 percent. The patient uses denial like a gambler to reverse the odds in his direction. Denial enables the patient to dismiss symptoms such as weight loss and pain as being serious but not fatal. One patient dying of leukemia had full knowledge of his condition, yet as death grew closer, he attributed his condition to the side effects of transfusion reaction and and psychic stress. According to Dr. Avery Weisman, "the primary reason that people use to urge denial is to fortify hope and prevent despair."[11]

A sixth insight into the experience of dying is in learning to speak of "an appropriate death."[12] This concept may seem strange for we have been reared in a culture that believes death is never appropriate. The medical profession have had a difficult time with understanding this idea because they have been taught in medical school that life must be saved at all costs. An ancient example of "an appropriate death" is found in the death of Socrates. Socrates did not wait until the end of his life to contemplate the meaning of death. His entire life was spent pondering the ultimate significance of life and death. When he was finally to die at the hands of the state, he did not panic or shrink from it. A variety of factors helped Socrates face death. One was age. He was seventy years old when he was sentenced to die. "When a man has reached my age," he says in Plato's *Crito,* "he ought not to be repining at the approach of death." He had done serious thinking about the meaning of death. For him it meant either the return of his soul to the realm of the ideas, a Socratic heaven, or to fall into a deep sleep. Neither option, he believed, was to be feared. His death was appropriate because he had resolved his basic conflict about death; having finished the business of living, he believed that death would not destroy the meaning or integrity of his life. The person who experiences "an appropriate death" accepts the reality of his own death with relief and resolution. It is death with meaning and dignity. It must be said, however, that what is appropriate for Socrates or someone else may not be appropriate for you and me. An appropriate death must be consistent with the values and meanings a person holds in life.

3. NEEDS OF THE DYING

The lessons and insights gained from those who have worked closely with dying patients helps us establish a style of ministering to the dying from the perspective of Christian faith. The ministry of the Church is to respond to the needs of persons wherever they are in whatever condition they are. Helping people to face and deal with death is a task not limited to the professional ministry—it is a task for the entire Church. We come to offer pastoral care, in the words of Carroll Wise, "the art of communicating the inner meaning of the Gospel to persons at the point of their need."[13] The primary form of communication will be listening, out of which we can respond to the needs expressed by the dying person—this provides the agenda. Too often the clergy have had a hidden agenda, sometimes to preach or pray or read Scripture. These things may be appropriate if they are asked for or if they are a natural response to an encounter. Our task is to listen and be responsive to a human being living through a difficult crisis.

A basic need of dying persons is for acceptance. This may seem self-evident for all persons have this need whether sick or well, but the crisis of dying brings about a crisis of acceptance in a special way. One cause of this is the isolation and loneliness experienced by dying persons. Another cause is the depersonalization of the treatment program where the patient feels more like an object or a guinea pig than a human being. When one is separated from other human beings and treated like a medical specimen, it is difficult to maintain feelings of integrity and worth. Frequently friends are reluctant to go to visit a dying person because they feel uncomfortable and "don't know what to say." It is important to remember that our presence is far more powerful than the words we speak. We can demonstrate acceptance merely by being with dying persons, being willing to stay with them and listen to them.

The dying also require an environment where reality is handled honestly. We may attempt to enshroud the dying in a conspiracy of silence, pretending that nothing of consequence is happening. A twelve-year-old girl with leukemia told the nurse that she was very tired and didn't feel like eating. The nurse told her, "Eat your food and take your medicine and everything will be all right." Another patient, a middle-aged man, told his wife, "I'm not going to be with you much longer. We need to get our business affairs straightened out." But the wife, unable to deal with reality of her husband's dying, changed the subject and talked about their plans for the coming summer. Those who have worked closely with the dying agree that their hardest task is to keep from putting obstacles between themselves and the patient. The problem is not so much that the dying are unable to cope with the knowledge of impending death; the real issue lies in the ability of those who work with the dying to be with them and not attempt to disguise the reality of the situation.

Perhaps the key issue is whether those who are involved in this ministry are willing to be in the presence of death. Our willingness to be with death will in large measure depend on our own attitudes toward death—our own in particular. In a death-denying culture we can easily develop sophisticated patterns of avoidance. Rather than involve ourselves in the process where death is being experienced, we make ourselves unavailable to those around us. One minister recalled that every time he visited a dying patient he felt faint. A seminarian went to see a friend dying of leukemia and was unable to recall anything that occurred during the visit. Those who have attempted to face their own anxiety about death and the kinds of avoidance patterns which are real for them are freer to be available to others.

A third need of the dying is to be able to express emotion and authentic feeling. The dying person experiences a wide range of emotions from depression and despair to relief and acceptance. Frequently the atmosphere this creates is testy and unpleasant. The ability to accept feelings expressed, no matter what or how, requires emotional stability and maturity. Many ministers seek to control an emotional outburst with spiritual and pious language and an attitude of otherworldliness; prayer and Bible reading are used as controls to keep a person in line. Nurses occasionally use isolation as a way of keeping patients under control. When the nurse doesn't show up for the bell or the normal services are overlooked, a patient soon gets the unfortunate message that he had better cooperate in order to receive help.

Finally, the dying person needs a framework for understanding what is happening to him. The question of life's meaning is no longer an intellectual issue. A sense of meaning must be obtained if the dying person is to not feel there is unfinished business before death comes. But how a person feels about death will in large measure depend on the sense of faith and meaning he has had in life, and I frankly doubt that this is a time to remake or restructure a person's theology. Some will disagree, feeling that this is the last chance we have to "save his soul," but I believe the pastoral care of the dying must emphasize a relational theology; that is, love and caring must structure our relationship with the dying person. We are the gospel, the bearers of good news. Our willingness to listen and be responsive is itself an affirmation of his dignity and worth. Our willingness to listen and respond to issues and questions of immediate concern is a way of enabling the dying person to deal with the crisis of meaning.

4. RELATIONSHIP OF LIFE TO DEATH

A death-denying culture attempts to separate life and death, to enshroud death in camouflage and silence. While a number of philosophies of life are present in our culture, two main views accomplish this separation. One looks at death with a stoic acceptance of the inevitable. This outlook is expressed in such slogans as "what will be will be" and "when your number's up, you've had it." At the other end of the spectrum is the glorification of death which claims that death alone gives true meaning to life. Whether a Socratic understanding of death as the beginning of true life, or Hemingway's life discovered on the brink of death, this point of view emphasizes death to the extreme that its opposite ignores it. Philosophically, we may speak of the first view as materialism or naturalism and the latter as idealism. The weakness of both points of view is that they do not see the dynamic interrelationship between life and death.

Naturalists look at life as a physiological process and death as the termination of the organism's biological function. Life and death are merely natural processes and must be understood as such; death is a universal law of nature, to which every organism is subject. And the life of man has no ultimate meaning since human existence is to be interpreted in and of itself. As Theodore Dreiser puts it:

Of one's ideals, struggles, deprivations, sorrows, and joys, it could only be said that they were chemical compulsions, something which for some inexplicable but unimportant reason responded to and resulted from the hope of pleasure and the fear of pain. Man was a mechanism, undevised and uncreated, and a badly and carelessly driven one at that.[14]

This, the underlying assumption of much modern medical science, helps to explain why some doctors work with a patient so long as life is possible, but when death is evident leave the patient alone. The physician is trained to cope with life, not death.

The idealistic approach to the relationship between life and death puts death on a pedestal. The classic expression of this view appeared in Greek philosophy in the writings of Plato, entered Christian thought in the second and third centuries, found a full-blown exposition in the writings of Augustine, and has been the general mood of Reformed theology from Calvin to the present day. Life is seen as a temporary sojourn from which only death leads to real life. The world is evil, and therefore life in it is essentially evil as well. Death comes to release us, to deliver our souls from the bodies that constrain them. The idealist sees death as the great liberator, coming to free in man that which is truly human— the soul or spirit—while the body is destroyed.

In biblical faith, life and death are not separated; instead an interdependent relationship exists between life and death. Man is a creature, and as such, his life is transitory and fleeting. "Man that is born of a woman is of few days, and full of trouble. He cometh forth like a flower, and withers; he flees like a shadow and continues not" (Job 14:1, 2). Mortal and finite, man comes from and returns to the dust. He is also, however, a unity, a creature who finds meaning in the totality of his existence. Man is not divisible into parts; he does not have a body and a soul—he *is* body and soul. Man in the Bible, just as in contemporary psychological writings, is a whole person. His unity moreover is expressed not only as a unity of body and soul, but also as a unity of dependence in his relationships with God, nature, and other persons.

The author of Genesis uses the phrase "image of God" to express man's unique creaturely relationship with God. In the ancient world a king frequently would place his image in provinces under his control as a reminder to the inhabitants that he was sovereign in the land. In like manner, the biblical writer sees man's role in the world as God's representative, here to uphold and enforce God's claims as sovereign Lord. As God's representative, man's special functions are to bring order out of disorder and to demonstrate divine authority over the natural world. Man's partnership with God causes him to share in completing the process of creation. To fail in this task is to sin, to move away from dependence on God, and to rebel against the task and destiny for which man was created.

Thus man is not a static entity, but a dynamic, growing being. Life is an ongoing movement involving every human being in coming out of a distant past into an unknown future. Man is a historical being—one who experiences life in an arena limited by space and time. Thus life must be dealt with in terms of attitudes toward past, present, and future. In a real sense, of course, we experience only the present. But the present is meaningful or empty depending on how we look at it. A meaningful present is experienced when we see our lives "standing within a dynamic development, a movement from a significant past, through this creative present, into a meaningful future."¹⁵ The present of the person who has meaning is experienced with expectation and hope, as well as with satisfaction and a sense of resolution. Faith as an interpretative act shapes the way we look at past, present, and future. Faith in Jesus Christ is a way of joining my personal history with history in general. Because the Christian claim is that Jesus Christ is the Lord of history, my personal faith in Christ enables me to see my past, present, and future joined with him. My destiny is therefore linked with God's purposes for history and his total creation.

Christian faith looks to the past to discover the key to an interpretation of history. This key is found in the life, death, and Resurrection of Jesus Christ. The claim of the Christian gospel is that

human history is a movement toward a final and complete fulfillment of the loving, creative purposes of God, and that God's love
for history and creation is definitively expressed in Jesus Christ.
Through faith in Jesus Christ God continues to lure men into a
community of freedom and love. This community, the Church, is
the context in which the question of life's meaning can be explored
and experienced. The Church attempts to keep alive and recreate
symbols of God's work in the past in order that the past might inform the present. The hallmark of past events is the Resurrection
of Jesus Christ. The first Christians found the meaning of life in their
experience of the Resurrection. The death of Jesus had brought
disillusionment and despair to his disciples. Their hopes that he
was the Messiah, "the one to redeem Israel," were crushed; their
belief that the kingdom of God had come in the power of Jesus'
ministry now seemed naïve and futile. Then an event took place
which vindicated Jesus' life and ministry, an event of such trans-
forming power that it brought hope out of despair, enabling the
first Christians to be "born anew to a living hope through the
resurrection of Jesus Christ from the dead" (I Pet. 1:3). Death
no longer threatened the ultimate meaning of human existence. In
the Resurrection of Jesus Christ the first Christians discovered
power and strength for daily living. The Apostle Paul, wishing to
discover this power for himself, prayed: "that I may know him
and the power of his resurrection" (Phil. 3:10). Resurrection faith
made sense out of the present as it found meaning in the past.

Christian faith also looks to the future in order to give meaning
to a creative present. It is not enough to find meaning in the past,
the future must also be seen as shaping the present. Christian faith
affirms that what God has done in the past, he can do in the future.
"Faith is grounded in memory but lives in hope. The victory has
not yet been fully won: but it shall be own in the near future!"[16]
Resurrection faith as a reality in the present gives hope for the
future—hope which consists of vision and promise. Christian
hope's clear vision for the future is symbolized in the phrase "kingdom of God," the final consummation of love and peace. *Peace,*
the word we use to translate the Hebrew word *shalom,* does not

refer merely to the absence of conflict, but to the final realization of the peace of God. This has been likened to the music of a symphony in which all of the individual notes, discords, and melodies alike are brought together and included in a higher harmony. Christian hope is that we will experience a time of fulfillment of the *shalom* of God. No more will there be death and suffering, no more war and turmoil among nations, no more murder and violence, no exploitation of the underdog—and, this vision of the peace of God's kingdom gives life meaning right now.

Furthermore, the Christian hope includes a promise. In the word "promise" we are ushered into the world of biblical hope. The concept of promise is prominent in the Bible, starting in the book of Genesis where God's promise to Abraham was expressed as the basis of a covenant relationship: "I will be your God and you will be my people." The promise of God provided the source, support, and destiny of the nation Israel. In the New Testament, the promises of God find their concrete expression in Jesus Christ, as Paul puts it, "For all the promises of God find their Yes in him" (II Cor. 1:20). A number of biblical images point the Christian to face the future with openness and hope. The Gospel of John speaks of the promise as eternal life. The Pauline writings picture God as one faithful to his promises, and notes that all who live by faith are the children to whom the promise is given. The author of Hebrews claims that through faith in Jesus Chrst we are heirs of the promise and this inheritance enables us to look at the present as a strategic time of opportunity. In the letters of Peter, the promise of God concerns the return of Jesus Christ and the final consummation of all things in him. These New Testament images not only invite us to face the future with hope, but to experience the present as a time of meaning based on the promises of God.

We cannot look at the future without realizing that death is a certainty. Death is one experience we know we will face in this life. Atheistic existentialists Sartre and Camus look at death as the decisive event declaring life to be absurd and meaningless; Sartre sees life as "the unbearable weight of existing," while Camus envisages life with its frustrations and hardships to be a reenactment of the

ancient myth of Sisyphus rolling his stone to the top of the moun-
tain only to have it tumble to the bottom again. For these two, life
is nothing more than waiting for an inevitable death. As Sartre
once put it, "nothingness lies coiled like a serpent at the heart of
human existence."[17] In my judgment these writers mistake death
and human finitude for the final index of the ultimate. Death
neither gives life meaning nor makes it meaningless. Instead, death
is the reality which confronts us with the question of life's significance. In the face of death we are concerned with our final destiny
and the fulfillment of those values and concerns to which we have
committed ourselves right now. Christian faith acknowledges the
crisis of meaning caused by physical death, but it does so in the
belief that through the Resurrection of Jesus Christ death has been
defeated. This faith perceives the power of meaning right now as
well as the hope of ultimate meaning in a life beyond.

5. POSITIVE VALUES OF DEATH

We commonly think of death in terms of its destructive force and
power. Death is an enemy, a catastrophic destructive force which
comes upon us, and we are unable to do anything about it. This negative outlook on death causes much anxiety and fear, and in some
cases, results in a paralyzing influence on life. Some people have so
feared death they have been unable to face life. Several years ago
some college students were asked to write down their thoughts about
death. One female undergraduate wrote, "Death is a very old
woman with horribly wrinkled skin and long, grey hair. She is a
very ugly person with a long, thin nose and thin lips."[18] Personifi-
cations of death as "the Grim Reaper" and "the Gay Deceiver"
illustrate our basically negative understanding of death. Fear of
death is normal, but there is also a morbid fear of death that drains
our energies and takes the vitality of living from us. While I doubt
seriously that many people would look upon death as a friend, it is
possible to indicate some of the positive values of death.

First, death makes it possible to evaluate the meaning of a
person's life as a whole. Life as we know it has two boundaries,

birth and death; therefore the final evaluation of a person's life must take place after death has occurred. We cannot make a judgment as to whether a life is good or bad, happy or unhappy, creative or wasted, without looking at the whole of it. If you had to evaluate the life of Adolf Hitler in 1912 when he was an unknown painter of shabby postcards, it would be far different than your evaluation of his life in 1945 after he had masterminded and carried out the plan to exterminate six million Jews. It is impossible to give an auditing of the book of life before it has been closed.

A second positive value of death is apparent when we see that the way a person dies may inform his life with special meaning. The act of dying can illuminate the end of life. Dramatically, we may think of this as the hero's or the martyr's death, but it also applies to the ordinary person who in the process of dying exemplifies special qualities. The young mother mentioned earlier who recorded her thoughts concerning dying sought to write a book on "how it feels to be dying and raising children at the same time." What she wrote was a deeply moving account of the thoughts and feelings of a courageous and sensitive human being. The final days of her life gave a sense of purpose not previously evident. Such an experience has been likened to the resolving chord in a melody. Certainly this analogy is applicable to the death of Jesus as recorded in the Gospels. The sacrificial nature of his life and ministry became even more apparent in his death on the cross. His teaching on forgiveness was given greater emphasis by the fact that he could forgive his enemies from the cross.

Third, our understanding of the present is interwoven with the fact that life as we now know it has an end. Existentialist philosophers like Jaspers and Heidegger have contributed significantly to our insights by defining death as a boundary which enables us to comprehend our nature as finite beings. Unfortunately our society behaves as though we were going to live forever, thus avoiding the issues of our finitude and mortality. We plan for the future as if it is endless while failing to face up to life right now. We look for meaning in our aspirations for the future or our recollections of the past. But the meaning of life is experienced in the here and now, a fact that death can help us deal with seriously and responsibly by providing our lives with a distinctive shape and character. In the awareness of our finitude and creatureliness we accept our humanity.

Fourth, death is a present possibility for my life. The simple truth is, I do not know when I will die. Every day I am involved in situations which may cause my death. Anyone who drives the freeways in America is aware of the possibilities of accidental death. A man in Los Angeles, the husband of a friend, stopped in a business establishment on his way home from work. While he was there, the store was robbed and he was shot and killed. The unexpected and precarious aspects of life are but constant reminders that we are not self-sufficient. A dam breaks and several hundred people are killed in the ensuing flood. A plane crashes and fifty people die. When I accept the fact that death is a present possibility in my life, I am able to affirm that life is precious and time is not to be trivialized or wasted.

Finally, death forces us to face the question of the meaning of life. A primary claim of Christian faith is that life as we know it in this world is not ended by final extinction. Death is the end of life as we know it, but it is not the end of our identity and consciousness as human beings. Through faith in Jesus Christ we affirm that death is not a final disaster but the beginning of what the Bible calls eternal life. Death is a positive reality because it thrusts the issue of meaning upon us. But death is not an index by which either life or the question of life's meaning can ultimately be interpreted. Life and death call for a larger, more comprehensive definition of meaning. The distinctive claim of Christian faith is that the meaning of death can ultimately be understood from the perspective of faith in a loving personal God who is known in Jesus Christ.

CHAPTER 4

The Significance of Death

To what does the term *death* refer? How are we to think of it? It is one thing to have an operational definition in order to tell when death has occurred, but what is it that has occurred? What is meant by the word *death* and in what ways is the term to be used? Perhaps these questions seem too theoretical, too philosophical for practical people. We have learned to think in terms of the here and now, and truth is not an abstract idea but something that works and can be experienced. After all, isn't death really a self-evident term? Don't we know instinctively what it means? A dictionary informs us that death is the act or fact of dying; the permanent ending of all life; the cessation of consciousness. Some philosophers have argued that we cannot speak of the term "death" in meaningful ways because we have not experienced it. Wittgenstein once observed: "Death is not an event in life. Death is not lived through."[1] And physicist Percy Bridgman argued that we could not speak of death in any clear way because we had not experienced it. If anyone had actually experienced it, Bridgman noted, we could not speak of him as dead. But this shut off any further discussion. It reminds me of the man who told a friend of mine in the midst of a heated discussion, "You don't know enough to ask the right questions." We may know very little about death, but to argue that we can say little if anything about it is a cop out. There are many things I haven't experienced that I talk about. And death is one experience that must be dealt with, no matter how partial our insight or knowledge may be.

We speak of death in a variety of ways. Death may be referred to as an "act," an "event," or a "process." We personify death with such phrases as "the Grim Reaper," "the Gay Deceiver," "the Gentle Comforter," or "the Dark Intruder." In more technical discussions of death terms are used such as "cessation," "termination," "interruption," and "continuation." To further complicate our difficulty in speaking of death we utilize a variety of poetic metaphors which have become a part of common speech. Thus it is not uncommon to find writers using phrases like "an appointment with death" or "a journey with death." Our rhetoric attempts to make death an object, a person, or an abstract idea. The language we use implies that we think of death as a thing or as a mysterious force which sneaks about in the darkness and comes upon us in strange and unexpected ways.

Those who have worked to provide an operational definition of death have been concerned to clarify the meaning of death in terms of complex issues brought about by medical technology and organ transplants. The matter of *when* and *how* death occurs is of pressing importance for those who work in a clinical setting. Yet it is both helpful and necessary to distinguish between a clinical way of using the word "death" and a theological understanding of death. The distinction is primarily one of focus and emphasis. While the clinician must deal with the *how* and *when* of death, the theologian is concerned with issues revolving around the *who, what,* and *why* of death. What this means is that while a theological understanding of death assumes that death is a dynamic process, it also means that death can be spoken of as an act or an event, so long as it is recognized that the terminology is dynamic and flexible, not static and rigid.

A theological interpretation of death is based on the assumption that life and death are a part of the same process and therefore it is possible to think of death as a termination process encompassing various levels or dimensions. While it is possible to separate the dimensions of death for the purposes of clarification, we should note that the levels are interpenetrating and interacting. The death event is the termination of the individual human being, the death of the whole person.

1. DEATH AS A PERSONAL EVENT

Death is a unique, personal reality in the life of every human being. It is the end of our human experience within boundaries of space and time and as such, marks the end of human life just as birth marks the beginning. There is significance, I think, in the fact that a cemetery marker indicates the boundaries of life by the date of birth and date of death. Birth and death are the parentheses that bracket the experience of each person. The fact that life can be experienced with meaning and purpose or as empty and without direction is intensified by our awareness of death. Death is a personal event because it is not something which merely happens to me; it is that which I actively experience. As the existentialist writers are fond of reminding us, no one can die our death for us any more than anyone can take our bath for us. There are some things we must do alone.

Recognition that death is a personal event implies that we must be willing to face death openly and realistically. My own death is of paramount importance to me. As we have already seen, it has the positive value of putting life in perspective, enabling us to sort out that which is trivial from that which is lasting, and setting a boundary on our lives which helps us to face the fact that we are mortal and finite. As a personal event death is not something I can share. Thus death is unique. It is different from all other events in our lives. For that reason it is the most significant event in life. All of us are aware *that* we shall die, but few human beings know precisely *when* death will come. Thus the factor of time shapes the human situation and effects the way we respond to death. Sometimes we attempt to avoid the personal nature of death by making it a generalized, public occurrence. The inner logic seems to be that that which happens to everyone in general happens to no one in particular. This is why the violence of films or the body counts of war or highway accidents have so little effect on us. We generalize death and thereby avoid the responsibility of personal application. So long as death is something that everyone else must face, I can deceive myself into thinking it doesn't concern me.

Another way to avoid the personal nature of death is to make it an abstraction. As an impersonal event death is stripped of its distinctively human quality. A dead body is not a person, we insist, but a "loved one" or a cadaver. Death as an impersonal event is of interest only to the pathologist or the statistician. To say that death is personal is to remove it from the laboratory and the formaldehyde. To treat death as an impersonal specimen removes it from what we know as the personal quality of life. Most of us want to live, to hold on to life. It matters very little if we call this the need to survive or life instinct. We experience life not only in terms of sensations and ideas, memories and hopes, we also experience life in terms of possibilities and opportunities, most of which are unrealized. We anticipate our next vacation or a trip to Europe. We await the realization of some future plan. The possibilities of life make it dynamic and open-ended. Life is continuously changing—it is characterized by growth and development. With the exception of those individuals who feel useless or want release from suffering or physical limitation, most of us hold on to life as though we cannot get enough of it. Death is a threat to life itself and so we remove it from the context of our personal existence. The ancient but questionable wisdom of Epicurus sounds all too familiar: "While we live, death is absent. When we die, we are absent, so death is simply nonexistent for us." This is the kind of impersonal abstraction that avoids the personal reality of death altogether.

Perhaps Martin Heidegger, the existentialist philosopher, has done more than any thinker in our time to force us to face the significance of death as a unique, personal event in life. Although the language of Heidegger is ponderous and frequently unintelligible, his insights are important to consider. Death is so central in Heidegger's philosophy that he speaks of human existence as "a being on the way to death." Death is far more than a biological fact for Heidegger. It is an element which shapes and molds human consciousness and concern. Man is not merely the being that knows he will die. He knows that he knows. It is man's awareness and self-consciousness that is the source of anxiety about death and human finitude. To deal with anxiety we make of death "the anonymous one," a generalized, impersonal force. The failure to see death in its personal dimension is the cause of inauthentic living, the kind of life that refuses to take time or the preciousness of life seriously. An authentic life is possible only when death is confronted as an internal, subjective, personal reality. When death becomes an imminent reality in life, every decision takes on new urgency and importance. According to Heidegger, our relationships with other persons are influenced by the way we deal with death. Only when we face head on the personal nature of death, says Heidegger, will we be able to understand the personal quality of life itself. To say that death is a personal event is to say that it is *my* death, the termination of *my* life, the cessation of *my* being. Because death is uniquely my own, it gives an unequivocal expression of the personal dimension of human existence.

What Heidegger stated in a philosophical way, the Russian novelist Leo Tolstoy put dramatically in his story *The Death of Ivan Ilyich*. Ivan Ilyich was a successful jurist who had mastered the art of superficial living and conforming to the "courtesies of social intercourse." When an insignificant injury turns to a terminal cancer, Ivan Ilyich's life is plagued with doubt and despair. He cannot accept the reality of what is happening to him. In a moving passage Tolstoy describes Ivan's dilemma: "Ivan Ilyich saw that he was dying, and he was in continual despair. In the depth of his heart he knew he was dying, but not only was he not accustomed to the thought, he simply did not and could not grasp it."[2] The struggle for prominence and success did not force Ivan Ilyich to face the issue of meaning and purpose in life. Not until the pain and symptoms of impending death came upon him did he deal with the personal nature of death, and even then, he could not fully grasp what was happening to him.

Tolstoy provides for his reader a vivid account of what happens to a man who refuses to take the possibility of his own death seriously. Family and friends, even the physician who cared for Ivan Ilyich, continued in a ritual that was finally recognized as nonsense and deception. Ivan Ilyich saw that the doctor was performing the same ridiculous ritual which he himself had performed as a jurist, listening to the speeches of the lawyers, pretending to be interested even though he knew very well they were lying. It was not until pain forced him to face "It," to deal with death as a personal reality in his life, that he was able to find an answer to his fear and anxiety. Only in facing the personal issue, "I am going to die," did Ivan Ilyich experience a sense of resolution and peace.

Recognition of death as a personal event in life, an event which may come at any moment, frees us to live an authentic and open life where meaning and purpose are integrally a part of living because death is a part of living. The personal dimension of death is therefore a controlling factor in shaping the fabric of life itself.

2. DEATH AS A SOCIAL EVENT

We cannot really say that men live or die as solitary individuals, isolated from other human beings. There is a sense in which the idea of the individual is an abstraction used merely for purposes of analysis and clarification. Man lives as a social being, dependent on other human beings and on an environment supportive to his growth and development as a person. Each human being grows in a community of persons who are mutually interdependent. After all, what could be more helpless than a tiny baby completely dependent for its life support on the family to which it comes? A primary problem for psychology is to discover the ways an unsocialized infant becomes an adult with specific loves and hates, loyalties and concerns, a person capable of taking his place in a complex structured society.[3] A sense of worth and dignity as a human being is developed in a social setting. And while every human being must die his own death, he does so in the context of a community that experiences death as the breaking of dependent relationships. The impact and power of death is experienced and realized in a social context. "Death is at once our defeat at the hand of the forces of nature and our final isolation from the community of the living."[4]

Thus it is not possible for us to think of the meaning of death apart from the social dimension. An essential element in defining what it means to be human is the acknowledgement that man is a social being. Personal identity and self-awareness develop in relationship with other human beings.

A man is a being who is bound with others as a fellowman. He is the being who exists not as an organism, by virtue of his birth, but as a fellowman, by virtue of his acknowledgement of others as existing over against himself and making his own life possible by their communications with him. His knowledge of himself as fated for physical death emerges in his life together with his fellowmen.[5]

Thus who we are and what we are willing to face in the future is part of the consciousness we develop with other persons. We die as human beings just as we live as human beings, in relationship with other persons in the world.

In the context of the social significance of death man's life as a dependent being is emphasized. Death separates a man from the community of the living and causes the dissolution of relationships in the human community. Cultural patterns of denial and avoidance are of social significance because they contribute to the ways men in community respond to death. The fact of death challenges the structures within a society, the organizational patterns within the society, the interpersonal relationships where a mutual interdependence is experienced on a daily basis, and the psychological impact which results from facing death and the loss of friends and co-workers. Death is the direct cause of the breakdown of man's dependent relatonships with fellowman, nature, and with God.

When we evaluate the social dimension of death we discover a basic reason for our fear and anxiety about death. The basis of all human community and the distinctive quality of life in community is love. Love of life is grounded in far more than the instinct for survival; it is based on the relationships in which love grows and is experienced. Death is the destroyer of love, and as such, is feared and avoided. We do not want to terminate relationships in which the very vitality of life itself has been experienced. Fear and anxiety is natural and should never be trivialized as emotional immaturity or lack of faith. The possible destruction of the relationships in which love is known is the basis of our fear. There is a true sense in which we can say, we do not fear death itself, but the destruction of community accomplished by death.

As a social event, death has a role and a social structure. One who dies leaves behind a number of vacant chairs. A family may be without a father, a business no longer has a partner, the church is without a deacon, the veteran's organization without a commander. A corporate identity crisis is brought on by death as social structures readjust and fill the place of the one who died. When a widow asks the question, "What will I do without him?" she is expressing the shock of facing a radical social readjustment. What American who witnessed the funeral of John F. Kennedy will ever forget the poignant symbols of the riderless horse and the jet formation with one plane missing. The empty chair is a vivid reminder of death's disruption. Social symbols have power because they point to a sense of loss. Death means that new roles are created—a wife is now a widow, a child an orphan, a couple is childless.

One of the first important studies of the social significance of death was the work of anthropologist Arnold van Gennep. Van Gennep noted that life consists of a number of transition experiences: birth, adolescence, marriage, retirement, and death. Most societies have developed rituals by which to express the meaning of these experiences, rituals called rites of passage. The rite of passage provided a symbolic way of acting out the inner meaning of these transition experiences. Each of the rites of passage were seen as having three movements or phases, described by van Gennep as the separation from a former state, the transition into a new state, and the incorporation into the new state. With the sacramental life of the Roman Catholic church, for example, each developmental stage of man is ritualized with a sacrament. Baptism is a rite of passage for birth, confirmation for adolescence, marriage marking the transition to family lfe, and Extreme Unction symbolizing the transition from life to death. While most Protestants have not used a sacramental expression, the concept of rite of passage is a meaningful way of speaking of transition experiences. The funeral serves as the basic ritual by which the transition from life to death is indicated.

A number of writers have pointed out that man alone celebrates death attempting to be "splendid in ashes and pompous in the grave"; man alone uses ritual to bury his dead. The answer lies in the social significance of death and the funeral as a social symbol. Yet in American society we are experiencing a deritualization of the funeral. Fewer people attend funeral services and a growing number of people want only to get it over with as quickly as possible. According to funeral industry personnel, the desire of growing numbers making arrangements is to make it simple and quick. While it is difficult to assess their total impact, critics of the funeral industry have undoubtedly caused skepticism and a lack of confidence in the value of the funeral. It is unfortunate that the critics have dealt primarily with the economic value of the funeral, for in my mind, this is far down the list of adequate reasons for affirming or denying the worth of the funeral. Ultimately the value of the funeral must be made in terms of the social dimension of death. A funeral is obviously conducted not for the dead but for the living. Thus the funeral should be evaluated in terms of the benefits it provides for the living, for the family and the community in which death occurs.

The funeral functions as a rite of passage in that it provides a ritualistic way of saying that a person who was once alive is now dead. This is why the entire funeral process can be significant. The funeral can be a means of reinforcing the reality of death. A family is forced to deal with death in the making of arrangements, attending the funeral service, and committing the body to a final resting place. The obituary announces the fact of death to the larger community. The cemetery stands as a social symbol for the community reflecting the basic beliefs and values of the community, as well as expressing what the living think of the dead. The symbol of the cemetery points to the new state into which the dead

have been incorporated and community rituals such as Memorial
Day symbolically express a continuity of the values of the living
and the dead.

As long as the cemetery is being filled with a fresh stream of the re-
cently dead, it stays symbolically a live and vital emblem, telling the
living of the meaning of life and death. . . . The symbols of death
say what life is and those of life define what death must be.[6]

But the value of the funeral is not only social, it is also psychological. The funeral provides an immediate context following death
in which the process of grief can be started. Basic research on
grief and the grieving process was done by Dr. Erich Lindemann of
the Harvard Medical School. According to Lindemann, "the funeral is psychologically necessary in order to give the opportunity
for 'grief work.' The bereaved must be given the capacity to work
through his grief if he is to come out of that situation emotionally
sound."[7] Not infrequently a funeral may provide a way of acting
out feelings which are of such high emotional content they cannot
be expressed verbally. Grief, essentially a deprivation experience,
results in a variety of complex emotional reactions—feelings of
anger, guilt, and bewilderment. Swiss psychiatrst Paul Tournier has
observed, "there is no grave beside which a flood of guilt feelings
does not assail the mind."[8] These feelings need to be manifested
in social interaction, and the funeral is one social context in which
they can be expressed.

If the funeral is to be psychologically valuable it must provide
for the bereaved an opportunity to face the reality of death and
the loss created by it. Facing death and the anxiety of separation
openly inevitably causes pain, but it is the kind of pain necessary
for healing. The funeral can be a vehicle for this kind of healthy
reality orientation. The process of making arrangements, selecting
a casket, visiting with friends, attending a service, viewing the
body, and going to the grave, can enable an individual to act out
and acknowledge his loss openly and with authenticity. Too frequently, however, the funeral industry personnel have created an
atmosphere of denial and have fostered only patterns of avoidance.

Viewing the body can be a healthy and realistic way of facing death. But when cosmetologists attempt to disguise the fact of death or make a person at eighty years of age look fifty, it promotes a bizarre, unrealistic setting.

The theological significance of the funeral is most clearly seen within the Christian community. The Christian funeral is a service of worship as well as a service of comfort and support for the bereaved. It is a way of expressing our gratitude to God for the gift of life, particularly the life we have shared with the deceased. Hearing the Word of God, in prayer, in singing, in meditation and spoken word, we proclaim that God is the author of life and the source of human good. We also affirm the worth and dignity of human life even in the face of death. And we express our hope that death is no final disaster, but that in Jesus Christ we are in relationship to the God of the living and of the dead. The funeral is the means of expressing the spiritual values and hopes of the Christian community.

3. DEATH AS A NATURAL EVENT

In facing the issue of whether death is a natural or unnatural event we come to a watershed in the history of Christian theology. This issue has been a point of distinction between Protestant and Roman Catholic interpretations of death. Traditional Protestant theology found its roots in the writings of Augustine who insisted that death is an unintended part of God's creation. The Augustinian tradition claims that death is unnatural because it was not a part of God's original purposes, but was the penalty levied as the result of man's sin. In this view, man was created in a state of sinless perfection enjoying complete fellowship with God, but disobedience in the Garden of Eden brought about man's Fall to imperfection and eventual death. Death entered the human race through the sin of one man and was then transmitted to all men.

The Lutheran tradition, represented by preacher-theologian Helmut Thielicke, strongly emphasizes the unnaturalness of death. Nowhere is death the expression of normality in nature. Instead, it is a catastrophe which is the direct opposite of man's intrinsic nature. The unnaturalness of death only becomes apparent when seen in the perspective of our relationship with God. Any attempt to look at man in isolation, apart from God, is the product of pride. God is the author of life, and death indicates that a divorce from God has resulted in ultmate disorder in creation. From the biblical point of view, Thielicke says, death is symptomatic of a mysterious distortion in life. Nature provides no analogies comparable to the psychological responses human beings make to death. Fear, dread, and anxiety are but symptoms of the unnatural character of death.

The Reformed tradition from Calvin to the present also affirms the unnaturalness of death. God created man a perfect being even though it was possible for him to sin. The first man Adam lived in a paradise, a state of bliss and fellowship with God, although fully aware that if he ate of the fruit of the tree in the midst of the garden, he would die (Gen. 3:3). After the act of disobedience man found himself in a state of sin, that is, it was no longer possible for him *not to* sin. The result of his sin was to be driven from the paradise of Eden and doomed to return to the dust from which he was taken. Fellowship with God was no longer a reality; man was now a sinner and the consequence of his sin was death, both physical and spiritual.

Both the Lutheran and Reformed interpretation are later versions of the Augustinian position. The assumption of Augustine, just as as for Luther and Calvin, was that the account of Adam's sin was a literal, historical narrative. Augustine added to the Genesis account that Adam was created in a state of original righteousness and fell through sin to a state of imperfection and unrighteousness. Whereas some early Church Fathers thought of the sin of Adam as the loss of fellowship with and good standing before God, Augustine thought of the Fall as a heinous, wicked corruption brought on by an evil will. Furthermore, he posited the view that sin was inherited physiologically from generation to generation, and the real source of human corruption was that human beings were the product of the inherently sinful sexual act. Thus death and sin were inherited by all the descendants of Adam.

Augustine and his followers based their interpretation of sin and death on Paul's discussion in Rom. 5:12–21. Augustine believed that Paul explained the origin of sin through physiological inheritance (even though this idea may also be seen as totally absent in Paul's thought). The descendants of Adam suffer two consequences of the Fall: first, an hereditary moral disease, the tendency to sin, and second, the guilt and punishment of Adam's sin. In Augustine's thought the Fall took man from a natural state of perfect fellowship with God to an unnatural state of sin and depravity which ends in death.

The Augustinian interpretation of sin and death became the official teaching of the Church in the Middle Ages. It was one important element in a larger theological framework described in Chapter Two. The Protestant Reformation brought a revival of Augustinian thought. And from the sixteenth century to the present the mainstream of Protestant orthodoxy has continued to teach that death is an unnatural event, the result of man's depravity and sin. All this is based on the view that Genesis 3 is a literal account of the first man, his Fall from perfection, and the transmission of his sin and guilt to all men.

Not all theologians agree, however, that death is an unnatural event. Renewed emphasis within Protestant circles has called for recognition of man's finitude and mortality as essential elements in the definition of what it means to be human. Dutch theologian P. J. van Leeuwen argues that "man as he was created was, and was willed and intended by God to be, a mortal being. We must deny that death is something unnatural, a break in God's creation."[9] But Karl Barth makes the strongest plea for our understanding of death as a natural part of God's creation. Two themes predominate in Barth's discussion; first, that the creation of God is good and under his sovereign control, and second, that man is mortal and finite. The goodness of God's creation means that even in death God is with us and for us. Finitude and mortality mean that the whole man experiences death. It is natural for a finite being to be subject to death. "Death is man's step from existence into non-existence, as birth is his step from non-existence into existence. In itself, therefore, it is not unnatural but natural for human life to run its course."[10] For Barth the term *natural* refers to that which is normal and expected in the ordinary course of events; thus death is the natural and expected end of finite human existence. This in no way infers that death should be looked upon as a friend or a kindly release from the sufferings of this life. Death is the enemy of man and the enemy of God; in fact it is the last enemy to be overcome and destroyed (I Cor. 15:26). When man looks at his finitude and eventual death, he does so in remorse and fear because he sees death as the seal and fulfillment of man's loss of being. According to Karl Barth, man's alienation from God causes him to fear death in this way. Death is looked upon as an enemy because we are fearful of God's judgment.

What is meant by death as a natural event will of course depend on how the term *natural* is used. One historical use came about through the legal use of the death certificate. The seventeenth century English courts were particularly interested in protecting the natural rights of a person. They also had the responsibility of assigning blame in the case of any death that was considered other than natural. In the case of a homicide or suicide, an inheritance would not be granted until the mode of death was clear and, if necessary, blame determined. When the investigation revealed that the mode of death was not by accident, suicide, or homicide, then a natural death was assumed.

What I mean in speaking of death as a natural event is that man as a bodily organism participates in the transitoriness of the material world. We are born and we die. I consider death to be a normal and natural part of God's good creation. Death is not to be understood as an exception to the creative purposes of God. We do not die because we must receive punishment for sin, or because we have inherited the penalty or guilt of Adam's sin. We die because we are human beings, creatures for whom death is the natural end to life.

4. DEATH AS A MYSTERY

Once we have examined the significance of death in the dimensions available to us—personal, social, and natural—we come to the dimension of mystery, and in doing so, enter into the world of the Bible. The biblical writers say surprisingly little about the nature of death, except that it is a stark reality each of us must face. Throughout the Old Testament, death is looked upon as the inevitable result of human mortality and finitude. The psalmist says that the mystery of death is expressed by the fact that death threatens the man of faith with the termination of his relationship with God. Death was a mystery to the Old Testament writer, in part because the continuation of life after death was but a dim reality. The Old Testament deals with the meaning of death in terms of man's relationship with God. Death is a reality "at the point where Jahweh forsakes a man, where he is silent . . . from there it is only a step till the final cessation of life."[11]

The predominating mood of Old Testament thought is found in the words of the psalmist when he asks: "What man can live and never see death?" (Psalm 89:48). Yet there are passages which express an uneasiness about death. Saul was "filled with fear" and "terrified" at the thought of his impending death (I Sam. 28:20, 21). His fear resulted from the threat of a premature or untimely death. Death is a problem for the one who is taken "in the noontide of my days" (Isa. 38:10), or "before his time" (Eccles. 7:17). The underlying view of man is that he is a creature, and as such, his life is transitory and fleeting. "Man that is born of a woman is of few days, and full of trouble. He cometh forth like a flower, then he withers; he flees like a shadow and continues not (Job 14:1, 2). But the mystery of death for the Old Testament writer is that death is not merely a terminal point at the end of life, but a power that breaks into man's present experience. The hidden nature of death is experienced in sickness, handicap, imprisonment, or the advance of age. The threat of death is an ever-present reality for men of the Old Testament.

It is significant that Jesus did not make death a central element in his teaching and preaching. It is difficult, if not impossible, to find a systematic handling of death in the Gospels. Jesus emphasized that the life of discipleship could eventuate in death, but even then the mention of death was merely to underscore the importance of the message. Emphasized in Jesus' preaching was the fact that death is an ever-present possibility for every man, and the knowledge of this fact should bring a man to repentance. When a man takes seriously both the precariousness and the preciousness of life, then he is ready to turn to God in repentance and faith. But death itself is a mystery in Jesus' teaching. He would not speculate on either the meaning of death itself or the nature of life after death. "What Jesus refused to say about death and life afterward is an important dimension of his understanding of man. Perhaps nothing he said is more important than what he refused to say."[12]

Jesus himself could not penetrate the mystery of death and when he faced his own death in the Gethsemane experience he was afraid. While he believed that his Father was with him, this did not spare him the agony of fear and sense of loss of relationship with God. A note of preparatory grief is evidenced in the statement: "I have a baptism to receive, and how distressed I am until it is over!" (Luke 12:50 *GNMM*). Both the prayer in the Garden and the cry from the cross indicate that Jesus did not take death lightly nor did he look upon it as a liberator or a friend.

Undoubtedly one element in the mystery of death is brought forth by the frequently asked question: Why do people die? Why is death a part of life? Why does it often come with such pain and grief and sense of loss? In answer to these questions many Christians have turned to the writings of St. Paul. We must remember, of course, that Paul was raised and trained in the Jewish tradition. As a first century Jew, Paul accepted the view that death is the result of sin, therefore any questions concerning the origin of death are inextricably involved with the issue of sin. Jewish tradition never questioned the view of a literal Garden of Eden and historic

Fall. Paul's discussion in Romans 5 is a theological development of the Genesis 3 account.

Since the basis for Paul's understanding of sin and death is Romans 5:12–21, it is valuable to trace the argument of Paul in that passage:

(1) Death, physical and spiritual, is the result of Adam's sin (vs. 12).

(2) Mankind stands as a corporate unity in relationship to God. Just as sin and death come upon all men because of the sin of Adam, so also the grace of God comes to all men in Jesus Christ (vs. 15–17).

(3) Just as sin and eventual death were a possibility for the first man, Adam, so also sin and death have been passed on to all men who are the descendants of Adam (vs. 18, 19).

(4) Sin and death came through one man, Adam, and they will likewise be abolished through one man, Jesus Christ (vs. 15, 17, 18, 19). It seems clear that Paul sees a causal connection between sin and death, yet the nature of this connection is undefined. While some commentators have claimed that Paul posits a basis for an inherited tendency to sin in this passage, and that this inherited tendency produces actual sins, a careful exegesis of the passage demonstrates that this is not the case. The passage contains a descriptive statement of the human condition. For Paul the ultimate origin of death and sin remains a mystery, although it is clear that he believed that death is in some way the actual result of sin.

It will be hard for some Christian people to accept, but at this point I believe we must simply admit that Paul was more closely in touch with his Jewish heritage and teaching than with the insights and claims of Old Testament revelation. An attempt to explain the relationship between sin and death by appealing to a literal interpretation of the Genesis 3 account is a denial of man's mortality and finitude. The fact that we are mortal and will eventually die is a given in any definition of what it means to be human. What, then, is the relationship between sin and death? An examination of the creation account of man in Genesis shows that man was made by God as a mortal being—"the Lord God formed man of dust from the ground . . ." (Gen. 2:7). No indication exists in this passage that man was a perfect being who lost his perfection. Even the curses mentioned do not speak of death but of life. What seems apparent in Genesis 2 is that man will become aware of his mortality and the implications of finitude if he sins. It is not merely that man is going to die; he knows that he is going to die, he can experience the "ego chill" which comes to those who attempt to contemplate nonbeing. Emil Brunner puts it this way:

It is not the fact that men die, that is the "wages of sin," but that they die as they do, in fear and agony, with the anxious uncertainty about that which lies on the other side of death, with a bad conscience, and the fear of possible punishment, in short, human death. We know no other death than this; we do not know the purely natural death of one who is sinless, and so sure of the divine that he sleeps away into eternal life. We know only the death of the sinner.[13]

Death is also a mystery for man in that no man can comprehend the death of the self. As we noted in Chapter One, Freud observed that none of his patients believed in the possibility of their own nonbeing. Freud saw this as a way of self-protection when confronting the mystery of death. The close interrelationship between life and death leaves the final significance of death in the arena of mystery. Nothing in our experience prepares us to stand the assertion "I die." We can dream and fantasize about life after death, but what actually happens at the point of death remains unknown to us.

Ultimately, the mystery of death calls us to be open to the future, a future which Christian faith sees as a part of God's creative purpose for man. From the perspective of faith, death is not an evil which inevitably evokes dread and fear, but a natural part of life; therefore, to be open to the future is to be open to death and what death will bring. Hope can be an anticipated practice for death, a hope against hope which refuses to rob death of its cloak. "Christian hope is not the attempt of reason to pierce through the future and so to rob it of mystery. The man who hopes is not making the irritating claim to know more about the future than others."[14]

CHAPTER 5

Life After Death

"If a man die, shall he live again?" (Job 14:14). The perplexing question of the author of Job continues to plague us. Since the beginning of recorded history, religion has been man's tool for alleviating his fear and anxiety about death. Is death the end of my mortal life? How can I die with so many hopes and dreams unrealized? What if I end not with a bang but a whimper? Some have suggested that the origin of man's belief in life after death is found in the dreams of those who have seen their fathers and friends die. The seeming reality and lifelike quality of the dream have been used as evidence to demonstrate the existence of a world beyond. It matters little whether the question is asked from the dreams of primitive man or the arguments of a sophisticated philosopher; the hope that death is not the end is real and vital.

Yet the hope of a future life is a frustrating and unresolved problem for modern secular man. In losing a religious framework by which to interpret the meaning of death, he has also lost a way of understanding life after death. Many modern theologians have abandoned a belief in a future otherworldly existence. Some speak of the symbols of the Bible as a way of opening the meaning and depth of our existence here and now. Paul Tillich puts the matter bluntly when he says that life after death is a "dangerously inadequate symbol" because it suggests the fanciful thought that there is continued existence after death—a concept he flatly rejects. In an age of skepticism about an otherworldly view of God, it should come as no surprise to discover belief in life after death fading away. In one of her seminars on death and dying, Dr. Elisabeth Kübler-Ross told the story of addressing a minister's group and asking them, "How many of you really believe in your gut that there is a life after death?" At first there was no response, and when she asked again, a trickle of hands were raised out of several hundred. Unquestionably, an enormous gap exists between theologians and the popular religion found in the churches. In congregations where a traditional theological framework is still adhered to, there seems to be no problem in expressing belief in a future life. Yet the gap between pastor and layman continues to grow, especially where there is no open conversation concerning issues involved.

This in no way implies that we have resolved our basic anxiety about death. As I have already noted, our death-denying culture is more anxious about death than any culture before us. We have not dealt with our anxiety but merely repressed it. The quasi-religious function of the funeral industry is possible because the needs of a public incapable of handling death must be met. The merchandising of funeral services, competitive advertising, hermetically sealed caskets, and perpetual care are merely external signs of a society that has substituted a future in heaven for eternal rest here on earth. We place our lifelike embalmed bodies in watertight, concrete vaults fully aware that it makes little rational sense; yet few of us deal with our anxiety in rational ways. Psychologist Erich Fromm observes that when future hope is lost, "the state of anxiety, the feeling of powerlessness and insignificance, and especially the doubt concerning one's future after death, represent a state of mind which is practically unbearable for anybody."[1]

And what about the incredible interest in religious experiences and psychic phenomena? Despite Bonhoeffer's claims that we are coming to a time when religion will be dead and despite short-lived cries that God is dead, religion is alive throughout America, and not merely within the confines of any small region. To be sure, expressions of religion do not always occur within the context of the institutional church, but a brief visit to any paperback bookstore is evidence enough of the vitality of religion. When theologians were embarrased to speak of a personal God and a life after death, people sought to deal with their spiritual needs by turning to horoscopes, séances, and transcendental meditation. Even *Life, Time,* and the New York *Times* magazine ran cover stories about the revival of religion. The Jesus movement returned to a literalistic view of the Bible and a strong emphasis on Christian hope for the future, using the biblical images of the Second Coming of Christ and the rapture of the Church. These expressions of religion are unexplainable, in my mind, without understanding that where there is strong anxiety about death, any means possible will be used to resolve it.

How can we speak of life after death in a way responsive to the anxiety of a death-denying culture? I must confess immediately that there is no simple or easy answer to this question. Earlier in this book I suggested that a theology of death must begin with Jesus Christ. The corollary to that assertion is that an adequate understanding of life after death must begin with the biblical witness of God's action in Jesus Christ. The biblical claim and the claim of historic Christianity is that death was overcome and defeated in Christ through the power of God. Jesus' Resurrection stands as the vindication of God's intention to destroy death. In Jesus we see God's promise that "the last enemy" will be defeated once and for all. We live now with death in our midst as an enemy and a destroyer. If death is the final end of human existence, the abolition and destruction of finite life, then death has the last word. In that case life would be defined by death. But if death is not the end—if there is a hope for a future life and the Resurrection of Jesus Christ is the key to that life—then death has no ultimate significance. We cannot make human death the criterion for determining the meaning of life right now or the nature of ultimate reality unless we are willing to make human existence the final index of what is real. The claim of Christian faith is that a God of unconditional self-giving love, known personally in Jesus Christ, is the index of the ultimate, and will determine the final outcome of life and death.

1. NEED FOR LIFE AFTER DEATH

One of the by-products of a society that has developed sophisticated gadgetry and technological wizardry is a fascination with the "new." The new is what is not yet—whether the "not yet" be a trip to Europe, a new experience, or some new gadget. Thus the future is defined by a society fascinated by the new and the novel as the "what-has-not-yet-been."[2] The future is contemplated as a reality and an experience that is "new" in the proper use of that term. Defining the future in this way has helped to create a consciousness where people experience what Kierkegaard called the "passion for the possible." In our time we have learned to utilize resources and opportunities available to us as building blocks, creative possibilities from which we make the future. This consciousness is the product of a secular society in which we feel autonomous in our ability to deal with and shape our world.

Theology has attempted to respond to this new situation and new way of looking at the future. Traditional concepts have been restructured in order that they might make sense to people in a secular age who have been so influenced by this new consciousness. This approach to theology begins with our concepts of God, who is not to be thought of as a being above or beyond this world, but as one who is "in front of us." The name of God given to Moses (Exodus 3:14) is put in futuristic terms, "I will be what I will be," the God who is before us holding the power of the future. The experience of salvation does not refer to deliverance from a future hell, but to a quality of experience in this life which will be brought to fulfillment in the life to come. Heaven is not thought of as a geographical location, but as a relationship with God in which the future fulfillment of salvation is experienced. These themes will be easily recognized by those familiar with the literature of the theology of hope.

Several important concepts are basic to this way of looking at the future and the meaning of Christian hope. First, no claims are made to present a blueprint or prewritten account of God's activity in the future. The Christian church has had from its inception groups convinced that they held the secret to what God is doing in history. We cannot use the Bible as a prophetic road map for understanding future events. What distinguishes this mood from that of Hal Lindsay's *The Late Great Planet Earth* is that no promises are made to provide the key to future events or to pierce the mystery of the future so central in biblical thought. We need to recognize the biblical claim that prophecy is like "a lamp shining in a dark place," not a chronicle of what to expect (II Peter 1:19).

A second theme taken from the theology of hope is that a theology concerned about the future must deal with the present. Theology cannot afford to be "escapist," to sit around waiting for Jesus to return on a white horse humming another chorus of "This World is Not my Home." Significantly, so-called "political theology" finds its roots in the theology of hope. Hope is an active, dynamic concept that revolutionizes the way we look at and think about the present. The Christian is a person lured forward and persuaded by the promise and the vision of God's kingdom; this is why he works for peace and the dignity and freedom for all men right now. The Christian believes the "good news" can be experienced and realized in the present.

A third theme of this theology is the trust in God with a future frequently mysterious and unknown. Christian faith claims that God can be trusted, even in the face of death. Death is not looked upon as an impassable barrier. "Christian hope has been called an anticipated practice for death, practice, that is, in a hope against all hope."[3] If God is the power of the future then we can trust in the future as we trust in God. Like Abraham of old, we face a new and unknown country. Our venture into a new land is grounded in our hope that the God of the future will be with us.

But why believe in a life after death? Can't we hold onto a dynamic faith without this aspect of traditional Christian belief? At this point I do not intend to present the arguments for and against the conviction that life continues after physical death, but I do want to list several reasons why I believe in life after death. It is possible to have a strong faith without believing that self-conscious existence continues after death. But for me such a belief is a primary affirmation of my faith in Jesus Christ. A casual reading of the New Testament and particularly the Gospels will indicate why belief in a future life begins with the biblical witness. The fact of a future life is a certainty in Jesus' teaching. Reference to a future life consistently recurs in the admonitions and warnings of Jesus to turn from evil and do the will of God. Jesus proclaimed an apocalyptic hope (that is, one emerging from divine revelation). Thus Mark's Gospel opens with the statement: "The (right) time has come, and the kingdom of God is near!" (Mark 1:15). The statement reflects the worldview of the first Christians—that there are two ages, this age and one to come, and that Jesus' life and ministry was the means by which the age to come had begun. The kingdom of God or God's reign became a present reality in Jesus Christ, and what we now experience is an overlapping of two ages; the age to come has entered this age, eternity has broken into time.[4] Jesus accepted the basic elements of apocalyptic teaching: the end of this age and an end of history; the reality of judgment; the reality of a future life with God. The details of these events were not elaborated in the record of Jesus' teaching, but it is clear that a life after death was an accepted fact for him.

A second reason for believing in a life after death is based on my conviction that in Jesus Christ we encounter a God of unconditional self-giving love. "Love never fails" is the teaching of the Apostle Paul, and it is difficult for me, if not impossible, to conceive of the love of God somehow being frustrated or thwarted. Christian belief in the goodness of life and the goodness of creation is grounded in the conviction that God is unconditional love. God created this world because it is the very nature of love to give. God involved himself with mankind because love is manifested as active involvement and concern. And God preserves and conserves that which is valuable because love seeks to bring that which is loved to fulfillment. God's involvement with man is not a temporary choice on his part. He decided to take man as his partner in creation and will not dissolve the partnership.

The need to believe in a life after death is important in any attempt to deal with the problem of evil. In speaking of evil I am talking about "that which frustrates or tends to frustrate God's purpose for His creation."[5] We can speak therefore of good as that which serves to fulfill God's purposes. The fact of disease which frequently brings untimely death and suffering is evil because it frustrates God's purposes for man. The destruction of war, natural catastrophe, death on the highways are frustrations of the purposes of God, particularly when the lives of capable people are cut short. The child cut down by leukemia or the family killed in an unforeseen earthquake are thwarted in their experience of the goodness of life. We may classify disaster as moral evil or natural evil, but that in no way changes the experience of tragedy in the lives of human beings. Evil is opposed to the purposes of God; it is inimical to that which is good, and the hope of man is that it will eventually be overcome and destroyed. Pain, suffering, and death are all considered as evils which will ultimately be overcome. God provides a context and an arena in which the struggle with evil and the development of persons can take place. Our world with its struggles and defeats provides one context in which this can take place. But this world is not the end of the struggle, and our human existence is not the end of what we experience. God's final and complete victory over evil is the hope of all who place their trust in him.

In the fourth place, my affirmation of a life after death is based on the conditions necessary to find meaning in life. In Chapter Three we suggested that we deal with this question from the perspective of a dynamic faith when we affirm that human history is a movement towards the final and complete fulfillment of the loving, creative purposes of God. We possess faith that points to the future, a future where death will be defeated and God's intentions realized for all men. This means that death is no final disaster, for God will have the last word. Hope looks forward to the time of fulfillment, a time in which the vision and promise of Christian hope and meaning will finally be realized. Life after death provides the time for hope to be fulfilled and faith to be completed.

2. IMMORTALITY

If it is true that death will eventually be overcome and we will experience a life beyond physical death, what kind of experience will it be? What can we know and understand about a future life? These questions manifest more than a basic anxiety that men have about the future. We will purposely limit this discussion to an investigation of major responses used by Chrstian theology. These have differed not only because of cultural and intellectual change, but also because the Bible itself says very little about the future in any specific or detailed way. When the first Christians wrote about the future life they expressed their hopes in a virtual collage of poetic images and symbols. Biblical writers were content to put their trust in God believing that what he had done in the Resurrection of Jesus Christ could be done in their lives as well. The focus of faith and hope was grounded in the nature and activity of God, not any substance or entity within the nature of man.

Through the centuries, however, Christians have been perplexed and frustrated by the thought that they do not know the precise details that take place after physical death. Unwilling either to admit frankly they did not know or to trust the future to God, they have made attempts to resolve the mystery of death. No proposal has been so popular or as widely used as the idea of immortality. While the term is basically imprecise, use of it implies that man does not really experience physical death because he is immortal. If mortality is life within the confines of space and time, immortality is life not tied to the limitations of this world.

There are two main views of immortality. Personal immortality refers to the survival of the individual soul after physical death. Used within the context of Christian theology, personal immortality affirms that the soul is not touched by the destructive power of death, but moves from time into eternity, from life here on this earth to life with God. Personal immortality emphasizes self-conscious, eternal existence after physical death. The second view, that of social or objective immortality, says that death affects the whole man, but the identity of man continues to exist in the mind of God. God takes man into his consciousness and awareness. Some would speak of social immortality in that our lives continue through the work we have done, the children we have borne, and the memories which others have of us. In no real sense is there a personal, self-conscious existence after death.

Two assumptions underlie the doctrine of personal immortality. First is the view of man as a dualism of body and soul. To be a human being is to be comprised of two substances, body and soul, and while the body is finite and subject to death, the soul is immortal and eternal. The second assumption is closely allied to the first; namely, death is defined as liberation, the separation of the soul from the body. Death brings release from the body, and through it the soul finds liberation from a physical body that has kept it in bondage.

Traditional Christian theology has accepted the concept of personal immortality as the most adequate way of understanding what happens to the soul at the moment of death. "It has always been the firm conviction of the Church of Jesus Christ that the soul continues to live even after its separation from the body."[6] This conviction is so deeply imbedded in the popular piety of many Christian people that if the suggestion is made that personal immortality may be an inappropriate and unbiblical way of understanding life after death, some gasp in horror and disbelief. Poetry used commonly at funeral services is saturated with the images of personal immortality. The poem "Resignation" by Henry Longfellow is frequently quoted:

> There is no death! What seems so is transition:
> This life of mortal breath
> Is but a suburb of the life elysian,
> Whose portal we call death.

Another frequently cited poem by John Luckey McCreery is entitled "There Is No Death":

> And ever near us though unseen,
> The dear immortal spirits tread,
> For all the boundless universe
> Is life—"there are no dead."

Poets have clearly seen how the doctrine of personal immortality can be used both as a way of accepting death while at the same time denying its reality and harshness. Another frequently quoted poem emphasizes the body–soul dualism basic to this conception of personal immortality, a poem called "The Tenant" by Frederick L. Knowles:

> This body is my house—it is not I:
> Herein I sojourn till, in some far sky,
> I lease a fairer dwelling, built to last
> Till all the carpentry of time is past. . . .
> This body is my house—it is not I.
> Triumphant in this faith I live, and die.

The doctrine of immortality of the soul finds its roots not in the world of the Bible but in the philosophy of the ancient Greeks. Plato first to cast the idea of immortality into a logically coherent system. His "proofs" for the immortality of the soul were offered as a direct response to the contention that the soul perishes with the body. Plato proposed a philosophical argument as a means of coping with fear and anxiety about the nature of death. He believed that fear of death could be alleviated if clear teaching concerning the nature of the soul were established. True philosophy, Plato claimed, was a practice for death because the philosopher is confident that he can find true wisdom only in the life to come. It would be folly for such a man to fear death.

In his dialogue *Phaedo,* Plato portrays the final scene in the life of his friend and teacher, Socrates. Socrates is discussing his now imminent death with friends. The dialogue is a vehicle for introducing Plato's "proofs" for the immortality of the soul. This last scene in the life of Socrates stands as the platonic model for the manner in which the true philosopher faces death with courage, confidence, and serenity. He is the true "death-accepter." Since death sets us free from the entanglements of the world of the senses and the world of appearances, fear of death shows that we care too much for the body and the pleasures of this world. Socrates shows that death is the soul's friend. What is real in man, his soul, experiences death merely as a moment of transition, a necessary door through which all men must pass.

Plato provides a means of answering the speculative questions surrounding death. Aware that his "proofs" do not offer an airtight argument for the existence of an immortal soul, he sought to demonstrate that death is an event affecting only the body since the soul is imperishable and cannot die. Only the body is corruptible and subject to death. Since the soul is immortal, death is defined as the separation or release of the soul from the prison house of body. What then is a proper attitude towards death? The courage and serenity of Socrates provide the best example for one who seeks wisdom. Philosophy teaches us to live in the face of death, acquiring understanding and insight by which the physical distractions and desires of the body are kept under control. True knowledge can come only when the soul is not impeded. Thus death is liberation, the freeing of the soul from a body which keeps it from functioning fully.

While it is not feasible for our purposes to trace the historical developments from Plato to the second and third century A.D., the period in which Christian theologians first began to use Greek ideas and concepts, it is important to note that this philosophical development culminated in a synthesis of philosophy and religion known as Neo-Platonism, which accepted the concepts of a body–soul dualism and the view of death as liberation. The overwhelming impact of Neo-Platonism on Christian thought may be seen in the attempts of early Church theologians such as Clement of Alexandria, Origen, and Augustine of Hippo to synthesize the two. The important result of this venture was that a theological understanding of death utilizing Greek concepts became the official teaching of the Christian church. The Platonic doctrine of the immortality of the soul was declared as dogma by the Lateran Council of 1512, accepted by Protestant reformers, incorporated into Prot-

estant confessions of faith in the seventeenth century, and continued as the basic way of thinking about life after death even to
the present day.

Belief in the immortality of the soul after death gave rise to interesting speculative discussions. If the soul left the body at the
moment of physical death and would not be reunited to the body
until the day of final Resurrection, where was the soul during this
intervening period? One alternative suggested that the soul was
active and another, passive. Augustine believed that the soul during
this intermediate state lived in a "secret storehouse," either resting
or in tribulation depending on how it spent its time in this life.
Thomas Aquinas, the medieval theologian whose ideas so influenced Roman Catholic thought, suggested that some souls spend
time in heaven or in hell while awaiting the final Resurrection. A
problem which emerged during the Middle Ages concerned the
matter of how a sinful soul could enter immediately into the presence of God, that is, capable of enjoying the beatific vision. In response to this problem the doctrine of purgatory arose, referring
to the state or place in which souls that will ultimately go to heaven
can be cleansed and purified of their sins in this life. Prayers for
the dead were developed to assist souls of those who were in this
time of purgation. Protestant reformers rejected that idea of purgatory but had no difficulty in accepting the doctrine of immortality
of the soul. John Calvin believed in the activity of the soul during
an intermediate state and spoke of "the watchfulness of the soul"
awaiting the Resurrection. The second alternative of the soul's
passivity was basically influenced by the biblical image of sleep as
a description of death. In one of his sermons, Martin Luther re-
marked: "We shall sleep until He comes and knocks on the little
grave and says: 'Doctor Martin, get up!' " Groups such as Seventh
Day Adventists have adopted the idea of soul sleep in an intermediate state. Basic to all of these discussions is the belief that the
soul exists independently of the body, a view that remained virtually unchallenged in Christian circles until this century.

The doctrine of immortality was used not only as a way of
conceptualizing the meaning of life after death; it also controlled

the definition of death itself. Immortality of the soul is a way of defining death so that death does not touch or affect the "real" person. Only the body experiences physical death, while the soul goes through a transition from this life to the life to come. The immortal soul is not affected; thus our attitude towards death should only be one of acceptance and serenity.

What should be our critical response to this way of thinking about life after death? My criticism is twofold: it is an unbiblical and unhealthy way of thinking about life after death. The fact that it is unbiblical is relatively easy to substantiate, but the conviction that it is unhealthy is far more difficult to back up, and takes me into the area of whether or not it is healthy to have a reality-oriented outlook on life. Nevertheless, I offer the following critique of the doctrine of the immortality of the soul. First, it is based on a view of man that comes from the world of Greek philosophy, not the Judaeo-Christian understanding of man found in the Bible. The biblical view—and I might add, view of man in the modern behavioral sciences—is that man is a psychophysical unity, a whole being, not a combination of parts. The whole person lives and the whole person experiences death. Second, the doctrine of immortality assumes that the hope of man rests in himself, in his immortal soul, while a Christian understanding of man sees that man's only hope is in the saving action of God. Christian faith looks on death not as a liberator or that which releases the soul from the bondage and pain of this world, but as an enemy, a catastrophic force which can only be overcome and defeated by the power of God. Third, the biblical and I would suggest Christian way to think of life after death is in terms of resurrection, not immortality. The New Testament uses the term immortality, but it does so to describe the nature of God (I Tim. 6:16) or the existence of man after the Resurrection when he will no longer be subject to corruption (I Cor. 15:42, 52, 54; II Tim. 1:10). Finally, the concept of immortality approaches death in categories which foster a climate of unrealty and denial. People are taught that death is something which really makes little difference. "There is no death," cry the poets who look upon death as merely a matter of appearances, a fiction in the minds of those who fail to see that the real part of man lives on. This trivializes death and robs it of its power. A form of intellectual denial, it keeps those who affirm it from facing death realistically. Accepting death is part of self-acceptance and few would claim, I suspect, that a healthy attitude towards life is possible without self-acceptance. How and what we think about the future makes an impact on the ways we live, think, and feel right now. Any attempt to deny the reality of death ends in a denial of the reality of life.

3. POWER OF RESURRECTION HOPE

We have made the claim that the theological starting point in a relational theology is in a dynamic faith in Jesus Christ, in whom we discover a way of understanding both the nature and activity of God as well as the meaning of being human. A corollary to that claim is that Christian hope is grounded in the Resurrection of Jesus Christ because through it God revealed himself as the power of the future beyond the finality of death.[7] Faith in the power of the Resurrection gives the Christian a hope for facing the future. Because of the Resurrection of Jesus Christ our attitude toward death is not one of acceptance or denial, but one of defiance. If the Resurrection is a reality we can indeed say with the Apostle Paul, "O death, where is thy victory? O death, where is thy sting?" (I Cor. 15:55). Death is indeed our last enemy, but God will speak the final word.

But why resurrection? The word itself may seem strange and primitive to many people, conjuring up images of dead bodies leaving their graves or other such bizarre happenings. The word "resurrection" is a metaphor, a term used to describe a new state of being, a totally different dimension of existence than anything known or experienced in this life. The familiar experience of sleeping and rising from sleep serves as a parable by which to understand the use of the term. In the New Testament three Greek words are translated "resurrection:" one means "to rouse from sleep"; another "to stand up" or "to rise up"; and a third means "to make alive." All of these words reflect the idea that resurrection is a response to the biblical conception of death as sleep. The hope of resurrection was a late development in the faith of Israel, one which grew out of Israel's need to deal with the question of evil and the justice of God during their exile in Babylon and later during the persecutions of the Maccabean period. An early expression of the hope of resurrection is found in Isaiah:

> Thy dead shall live, their bodies shall rise.
> O dwellers in the dust, awake and sing for joy!
> *Isa. 26:19*

But this is a corporate hope for the nation. It is not until later that the individual hope of resurrection is expressed in Daniel 12:2: "And many of those who sleep in the dust of the earth shall awake, some to everlasting life, and some to shame and everlasting contempt." These statements were to affirm that God's justice would be realized and death would not be a limit to the realization of God's purposes. By the time of Jesus' life and ministry in Palestine, the idea of resurrection was well known. It became a matter of heated debate between the Pharisees and the Sadducees, the latter group rejecting the idea completely. The themes of the kingdom of God, the coming judgment, and the Resurrection were important elements in Jesus' teaching. A complete examination of the New Testament use of resurrection can be divided into three main areas: the Resurrection of Jesus; the meaning of resurrection in the life of faith now; and the meaning of resurrection in the age to come.

Resurrection of Jesus

The central focus of New Testament faith is the Resurrection of Jesus. The only documents of Jesus' life we possess, the four Gospels, paint the story of Jesus in the colors of Easter. All four Gospels emphasize that the tomb was empty, that he appeared to his disciples, and that the disciples believed that he had risen from the dead. The Book of Acts records the early preaching of the Church with its emphasis on the Resurrection. When Paul went to

Athens, the stronghold of Greek philosophy and the belief in immortality of the soul, he "preached Jesus and the resurrection" (Acts 17:18). And in his letter to the Corinthian church, he again expressed the central importance of the Resurrection: "If Christ has not been raised, your faith is futile. . . . If in this life we who are in Christ have only hope, we are of all men most to be pitied" (I Cor. 15:17, 19). The witness of the New Testament is quite clear: without the Resurrection there is no basis for faith or hope.

The biblical witness to the Resurrection of Jesus confronts us with two issues basic to a theological understanding of death. First, the claim of the New Testament and the early Church is that the Resurrection actually happened, and second, the event of the Resurrection has meaning in terms of God's creative activity and purposes. A great deal of discussion amongst theologians involves the first point. Some theologians claim that the very idea of resurrection from the dead makes no rational sense in a scientific world; therefore if we are to speak of it at all we must do so only in terms of personal meaning. On scientific grounds we know that it could not happen, argue those who discount it on rational grounds, but the first followers of Jesus lived in a prescientific world which did not question the possibility of miraculous events. They believed in the Resurrection and thus gave it meaning.

On the opposite side of the discussion are those who claim not only that the Resurrection actually happened, but that it is an historical event that can be documented, analyzed and understood; we possess New Testament documents bearing witness to the fact of the Resurrection and these can be used to establish a historically verifiable foundation.

In my mind both positions represent extremist points of view. The Resurrection of Jesus actually happened—on this I am not willing to equivocate. But to claim it is capable of being analyzed and understood in the same way we deal with other historical events is to fail to see the uniqueness of the Resurrection. To be sure a framework of events make up its nexus. We are talking about an historical person, Jesus of Nazareth, and we are claiming that he was raised from death at a specific time: after the Crucifixion and before he was seen by his disciples. We are also claiming that these events occurred in a specific place, Jerusalem. There were no eyewitnesses to the Resurrection itself, that is, no one actually saw the event take place. Therefore, we must frankly admit that we are dealing with the testimonies of men who saw Jesus after the Resurrection and went about proclaiming that fact.

We cannot verify the Resurrection historically not only because no witnesses observed the event, but because the event itself is unique; it is completely new—different from anything before or since in the course of human history. This brings us to the second issue concerning the meaning of Jesus' Resurrection; it marked the beginning of a new dimension in the creative purposes of God. The Resurrection marked the breakthrough to a new dimension of reality, a step forward in the spiritual development of man. Through the Resurrection the age to come broke upon this age and the age of the Spirit was inaugurated. The last event in Jesus' life; it is the new beginning moving man beyond negation of life. The Resurrection of Jesus was God's first step in the destruction of death. The last enemy was conquered in the life of Jesus as an anticipation of the future, a glimpse into the dimension where hope will be realized. The Apostle Paul expressed this when he spoke of the Resurrection as "the first fruits" (I Cor. 15:23). Throughout the discussion in this chapter of I Corinthians, Paul places great emphasis on the fact that the Resurrection is new and unique. I think it is possible to see an analogy between the Resurrection of Jesus and that point in the process of evolutionary development when life first emerged from what was previously all matter. With the first living cell a new dimension of reality was ushered in. Likewise with the Resurrection of Jesus a new dimension, a new creation, was inaugurated.

The Resurrection of Jesus is also the confirmation of Jesus' life, ministry, and death on the cross. During his ministry as recorded in the Gospels, Jesus made startling claims about who he was and what he was doing. These claims resulted in his death. He was considered to be a blasphemer by the Jewish religious leaders and a political rebel by the Roman governor. The first preachers of the gospel offered this interpretation of the Resurrection: they declared that by this act God put his stamp of approval on Jesus' divine mission. These preachers claimed that the Resurrection validated Jesus' claim to be Lord and Christ (Acts 2:36; 5:30, 31); indeed, they said he was the Messiah of Israel and the coming Son of Man—powerful symbols to the Jewish community. These claims, implicit in Jesus' teaching and in his death on the cross, became explicit through the Resurrection.

In a third meaning of the Resurrection, Jesus is affirmed as the one in whom and through whom God makes himself known. After the Resurrection Paul could say, "God was in Christ reconciling the world to himself" (II Cor. 5:19), a statement that would have had little meaning before hand. In Jesus Christ we discover God to be the God of promise, the God of the future, the God who conquers and overcomes the power of death. The power of the Resurrection is no mere brute fact that Jesus rose from the dead, but that he is risen to reveal that God is a God of the living and not of the dead.

Resurrection Experience

Does the power of the Resurrection make any difference in our lives right now? In what ways can the experience of faith and hope be an experience of the Resurrection? These are important questions for a relational theology as they were important to the first Christians. We have said that the event by which Jesus moved from death to new life was called Resurrection, the breaking in of a new dimension of reality, the experiencing of new creation. Much of Christian theology has dealt with the Resurrection only in terms of past and future: the Resurrection of Jesus and the general Resurrection which is to come. This emphasis on past and future has robbed the Resurrection of its power in the present.

The writers of the New Testament were concerned about the resurrection experience and did not hesitate to speak of it. In Rom. 6:4 Paul speaks of the resurrection experience as walking in "newness of life" and indicates that this is part of the symbolism of baptism. Baptismal imagery is a part of Col. 2.12 and is the background for the discussion of the risen life in Col. 3:1ff. A similar theme is found in Eph. 2:4ff. And in I Pet. 1:3 we are told that "we have been born anew to a living hope through the resurrection of Jesus Christ from the dead." But what is the meaning of this Biblical language and how do we translate it into terms which will give insight into our experience right now?

In a sense the experience of resurrection is always a miracle— not in the older use of the word as a suspension of natural law, but miracle defined as a new creative act, an experience of novelty, the never-before-known. To be experienced as miracle an act must be perceived with wonder and awe. Apart from the sense of wonder the extraordinary can be commonplace. The Christmas story reminds us of this; the skeptic could go to Bethlehem completely unimpressed, seeing only a poor family in an out of the way place. Not so the shepherds and the Magi, who seeing the baby Jesus "fell down and worshiped him" (Matt. 2:11). It is significant that the ten recorded appearances of the resurrected Christ were experienced only by those who believed. No skeptic saw the risen Lord, and no one who considers the Resurrection in cynicism and contempt will experience the power of the resurrection experience. The miracle will most frequently be discovered in the ordinary experiences of life. I know a couple who discovered that after fifteen years their marriage was stale and stagnant; now, after a time of separation and evaluation, they have experienced the miracle of resurrection in their marriage. I have seen dried up artists who have lost the creative spirit after an experience of new life begin to rediscover their talents and move on to new plateaus of creative work. I have spoken with people having no sense of meaning or direction in their lives who accepted the claims of Jesus Christ and joined the exciting pilgrimage of new life with him, finding purpose and hope in living. It matters very little how or where the experience of resurrection comes, what matters is that we are willing to receive it as God's gift.

Some Christian people are bothered if an experience like resurrection is spoken of in the language of human relationships. It is assumed, somehow, that resurrection is a specal miracle of God that "zaps" us like a bolt of lightning. It certainly can happen that way, but it also comes in common and ordinary ways and we should not close ourselves off from it. We need to be aware of the fact that the time and place of a resurrection experience cannot be controlled. We may find resurrection in a secular setting totally apart from the life of the Christian community. Many people in our day are experiencing new life in the human potential movement. through the medium of sensitivity or encounter groups or experiences where feeling and bodily awareness are emphasized. Many have found life and hope in psychotherapy. Why should we say these experiences are not "Christian" or suggest that the new life found in them is not genuine resurrection? Perhaps we need to be reminded that God can work through any person or method he desires to use, even an uneducated carpenter from Nazareth. New life and new hope, so much a part of the resurrection experience, cannot be compartmentalized or controlled.

When we talk about the Christian doctrine of Resurrection, we are speaking of the Resurrection of the body. We have already noted that a biblical view of man understands man as a unified being, a psychosomatic unity, not a soul contained within a body. Resurrection, therefore, is the bringing of the new creation to the whole man, the total person. This means we dare not exclude the physical body in the experience of resurrection, particularly the sexual relationship. I am not implying that sexuality is essentially a physical or bodily function, but a negative view of the body generally results in an unhealthy outlook on our sexuality. Many Christian people have never discovered a healthy, wholesome outlook on the sexual relationship, having accepted the view that sex is bad and sexual intercourse sinful. Augustine's teaching on the sinfulness of the sexual act has had a lasting impact on the Christian Church and its teaching about human sexuality. Any pastoral counselor will inform you that marriages break down because of the inability of couples to relate sexually. Do problems like premature ejaculation or inability to achieve orgasm have anything to do with the Christian understanding of resurrection? I am unwilling to exclude theology from problems so important to people they will pay $2,500 to Masters and Johnson to find help. These people need to experience the resurrection of the body, the experience of the body being raised to new levels of potential and creativity and fulfillment.

When the Apostle Paul spoke of the qualities of the resurrection experience in the life of faith, he did so in terms which describe new life in human relationships. The resurrection experience included qualities such as "compassion, kindness, lowliness, meekness, and patience" (Col. 3:12, 13). The concrete experience was of new life and new creation, not of ideals expressing the hope of good news but the living of good news in the everyday experiences of life. The Christian claim of resurrection is that it is "a living hope," a dimension of life experienced right now in our feelings about ourselves and in the way we act and relate to other persons. Resurrection grows in relationship—in a dynamic faith in Jesus Christ through whom the new creation becomes a present reality and in our relationships with other persons with whom this new reality is experienced.

Future Resurrection

A dynamic faith is incomplete without the conviction that in the future God will bring to completion his creative purposes for mankind and the entire created order. Themes which comprise the doctrine of "last things" in the New Testament include the kingdom of God, the end of history, the second coming of Jesus Christ, the general Resurrection of the dead, the Last Judgment, heaven and hell, and the final victory of God. These images and symbols make up the New Testament hope for the future. They point to the final consummation of all things, including a solution to the problem of evil, the defeat of death, an ultimate fulfillment for all human beings, and the completion of God's creative work. All of this is based on the faith that a God of unconditional self-giving love will complete that which he has begun. The issue of the future is the nature and purpose of God. "God is the power of the future. God is the power of the new."[8]

Resurrection is God's answer to the problem of death. The

biblical witness is clear that when we ask questions about the nature of the Resurrection we can ask about the "who" and "that" but not the "how" and "when." A systematic account of the future Resurrection by Paul appears in I Corinthians 15. The "who" of resurrection is the living God who raises the dead by his own power (vs. 15, 38, 57). The "that" of resurrection is affirmed throughout the passage, specifically, that what God did in Jesus Christ in overcoming death, he will do for all men at the end of the age. But with regard to the interesting speculative questions about "when" all of this might occur, or "how" it is going to take place, Paul is silent. The discussion does contain an intriguing analogy concerning the nature of the Resurrection body. In I Cor. 15:35–50 Paul argues that the physical body which experiences death will be raised a "spiritual body," the argument based on the statement in vs. 50, "flesh and blood cannot inherit the kingdom of God, nor does the perishable inherit the imperishable." At the heart of Paul's discussion is the contention that there is nothing "natural" about the Resurrection; that is, it is unique and new, something only God can bring about. Thus the doxology in vs. 57 —we are participants in a victory over death and it is God who accomplishes this victory in us.

This whole discussion of resurrection makes evident that a Christian understanding of resurrection as a way of conceptualizing the meaning of life after death is certainly not more rational or intellectually easier to accept than other formulations. "For the claim of the doctrine of resurrection is that only because of what God does have men reason to believe in a life after death, not because of what man is."[9] The doctrine of resurrection is a promise that calls us to faith and obedience. The life of faith always contains risk and more often than not will create a sense of insecurity. The person looking for details about the future, "the furniture of heaven and the temperature of hell," will inevitably find frustration. I feel confident that all this will be equally frustrating to one who in the name of rationality and freedom is convinced still too much is left to faith. I have purposely left questions unanswered. What kind of experience will a life after death entail? Will we be self-conscious and aware in a similar sense to our experience in this life? If Jesus said he is going to "prepare a place" for us (John 14:1, 2), what does that mean? Will we "see" God? The questions are laden with the baggage of space and time—even our language is bound by the world of objects, things, and the succession of minutes on the clock.

The claim of Christian hope is that we will someday know even as we now are known (I Cor. 13:12), and that experience holds the promise of a full and complete relationship with God. Perhaps the best we can do is cling to the vision of the Book of Revelation:

Behold, the dwelling of God is with men. He will dwell with them, and they shall be his people, and God himself will be with them; he will wipe away every tear from their eyes, and death shall be no more, neither shall there be mourning nor crying nor pain any more, for the former things have passed away.

Rev. 21:3, 4

If all that we have claimed about a God of unconditional self-giving love is true, then we can trust him with our future.

Notes

INTRODUCTION

1. Quoted in *The New Yorker*, March 22, 1969, p. 31.
2. *The Theology of Hope*, tr. James W. Leitch (New York: Harper & Row, 1967), p. 16.
3. Robert Neale, *In Praise of Play* (New York: Harper & Row, 1969), p. 168.

CHAPTER I

1. Toynbee, ed. *Man's Concern With Death* (New York: McGraw-Hill Book Company, 1968), p. 131.
2. Fulton, ed. *Death and Identity* (New York: John Wiley and Sons, Inc., 1965), p. 4.
3. *Death, Grief, and Mourning* (New York: Anchor Books, 1967), pp. 192–199.
4. *The Meaning of Immortality in Human Experience* (New York: Harper & Row, 1957), p. 5.
5. Feifel, ed. *The Meaning of Death* (New York: McGraw-Hill Book Company, 1959), p. xii.
6. "Thoughts for the Times on War and Death," (1915) *Collected Papers* (New York: Basic Books, 1959), volume 4, p. 305, 306.
7. *On Death and Dying* (New York: The Macmillan Company, 1969), p. 12.
8. Alan Harrington, *The Immortalist* (New York: Avon Books, 1969), p. 217.
9. Paul Irion, *The Funeral: Vestige or Value?* (Nashville: Abingdon Press, 1966), pp. 20–43.

10. "Explorations in Death Education," *Pastoral Psychology* (November, 1971), p. 35.
11. Ibid.
12. *The American Way of Death* (New York: Simon and Schuster, 1963), p. 17.
13. Op. cit., pp. 44–51.
14. For a complete discussion of this issue, see Paul Ramsey, *The Patient as Person*. New Haven: Yale University Press, 1970.
15. J. William Worden, "The Right to Die," *Pastoral Psychology* (June, 1972), pp. 9–14.

CHAPTER II

1. Gorden Kaufman, *Systematic Theology: A Historicist Perspective* (New York: Charles Scribner's Sons, 1968), p. ix.
2. *Faith and Knowledge* (Ithaca, N.Y.: Cornell University Press, Second Edition, 1966), p. 217.
3. Richard W. Doss, "Towards a Theology of Death," *Pastoral Psychology* (June, 1972), pp. 16–18. See also "Developing a Theology of Death," *Foundations* (July–Sept., 1971), pp. 224–235.
4. Edward J. Young, *Thy Word Is Truth* (Grand Rapids, Mi.: William Eerdman's Publishing Company, 1957), p. 5.
5. Ibid., p. 166.
6. *Institutes of the Christian Religion,* tr. John T. McNeill (Philadelphia: The Westminster Press, 1957), III, ix, 4.
7. Lorraine Boettner, *Immortality* (Grand Rapids, Mi.: William B. Eerdman's Company, 1956), p. 23.
8. Book 13, chapter 3.
9. Boettner, op. cit., p. 18.
10. Ibid., p. 35.
11. Charles Hartshorne, *The Logic of Perfection* (La Salle, Ill.: (Open Court Publishing Company, 1962), p. 253.
12. *The Phenomenon of Man,* tr. Bernard Wall (New York: Harper Torchbooks, 1965), p. 283.
13. E. R. Hardy, ed. *Christology of the Later Fathers* (Philadelphia: The Westminster Press).
14. *Letters and Papers from Prison,* tr. Reginald Fuller (New York: The Macmillan Company, 1967), p. 201.

CHAPTER III

1. From *The Myth of Sisyphus.* Quoted in Ignace Lepp, *Death and Its Mysteries,* tr. Bernard Murchland (New York: The Macmillan Company, 1968), p. 132.

2. *Psychology and the Human Dilemma* (New York: D. Van Nostrand Company, 1967), p. 25.
3. Robert Kastenbaum and Ruth Aisenberg, *The Psychology of Death* (New York: Springer Publishing Company, 1972), p. 55.
4. Op. cit., p. 41.
5. *On Death and Dying,* p. 34ff.
6. E. Mansell Pattison, "Afraid to Die," *Pastoral Psychology* (June, 1972), pp. 41–51.
7. John Hinton, *Dying* (New York: Penguin Books, 1967), p. 77.
8. Op. cit., pp. 25–29.
9. Ibid., p. 27.
10. Avery Weisman, "On The Value of Denying Death," *Pastoral Psychology* (June, 1972), pp. 24–32.
11. Ibid., p. 30.
12. Avery D. Weisman and Thomas P. Hackett, "Predilection to Death," *Death and Identity,* ed. Robert Fulton (New York: John Wiley and Sons, 1965), pp. 319–328.
13. *The Meaning of Pastoral Care* (New York: Harper & Row, 1966), p. 8.
14. Quoted in Liston O. Mills, ed. *Perspectives on Death* (Nashville: Abingdon Press, 1969), p. 143.
15. Gorden Kaufman, op. cit., p. 347.
16. Ibid., p. 400.
17. *Being and Nothingness,* tr. Hazel Barnes (Philosophical Library, 1956), p. 21.
18. Kastenbaum and Aisenberg, op. cit., p. 155.

CHAPTER IV

1. Ludwig Wittgenstein, *Tractatus Logico-Philosophicus* (Kegan Paul, 1922), p. 185.
2. (New York: A Signet Classic of the American Library), p. 131.
3. Gorden W. Allport, *Becoming* (New Haven: Yale University Press, 1955), p. 29.
4. John Macmurray, *Persons in Relation* (Faber & Faber, Ltd., 1957), p. 165.
5. Joseph Haroutunian, "Life and Death Among Fellowmen, " *The Modern Vision of Death,* ed. Nathan A. Scott, Jr. (Richmond: John Knox Press, 1967), p. 86.
6. W. Lloyd Warner, *The Living and the Dead* (New Haven: Yale University Press, 1959), pp. 380, 381.
7. Erich Lindemann, "Symptomatology and Management of Acute Grief," *Death and Identity,* ed. Robert Fulton (New York: John Wiley & Sons, Inc., 1965), pp. 186–201.

8. *Guilt and Grace,* tr. Arthur W. Heathcote (New York: Harper & Row, 1962).
9. Quoted in G. C. Berkouwer, *Man: The Image of God* (Grand Rapids, Mi.: William Eerdmans Company, 1962), pp. 199, 200.
10. Karl Barth, *Church Dogmatics,* III, 2, tr. J. K. S. Reid (T & T Clark, 1960), p. 625.
11. Gerhard von Rad, *Old Testament Theology,* volume 1, tr. D. M. G. Stalker (New York: Harper & Row, 1962), p. 388.
12. Leander Keck, "New Testament Views of Death," *Perspectives on Death,* ed. Liston O. Mills (Nashville: Abingdon Press, 1969), p. 43.
13. *The Christian Doctrine of Creation and Redemption,* tr. Olive Wyon (Philadelphia: The Westminster Press, 1952), pp. 129, 130.
14. Johannes B. Metz, "Creative Hope," *New Theology No. 5,* ed. Martin E. Marty and Dean G. Peerman (New York: The Macmillan Company, 1968), p. 141.

CHAPTER V

1. *Escape From Freedom* (New York: Avon Books, 1965), p. 110.
2. Johannes B. Metz, *Creative Hope,* p. 131.
3. Ibid., p. 141.
4. This concept is more fully explained in Oscar Cullmann, *Christ and Time,* tr. Floyd V. Filson (Philadelphia: The Westminster Press, 1950), pp. 81–93.
5. John Hick, *Evil and the God of Love* (New York: Harper & Row, 1966), p. 374.
6. Louis Berkhof, *Systematic Theology* (Grand Rapids, Mi.: William B. Eerdmans Co., 1959), p. 672.
7. Carl Braaten, *The Future of God* (New York: Harper & Row, 1969), p. 73.
8. Jürgen Moltmann, *Religion, Revolution and the Future,* tr. M. Douglas Meeks (New York: Charles Scribner's Sons, 1969), p. 61.
9. Kaufman, *Systematic Theology,* p. 467.

Index

Fromm, Erich, 76
Fulton, Robert, 3
Funeral, 11–13, 65, 76

God, 23f.
   personal, 56
   unconditional love of, 32, 33, 77,
      78, 80, 97
Gorer, Geoffrey, 3, 9
Grief, 13, 66

Harmer, Ruth, 11
Heidegger, Martin, 55, 60f.
Hick, John, 20
Hitler, Adolf, 55
Hocking, William Ernest, 3
Hope, 35, 53, 74, 75, 78f., 88, 94,
   95, 97

Image of God, 51
Immortality, 5, 6, 82f.
Irion, Paul, 12

Jaspers, Karl, 55
Jesus Christ, 19, 20, 24, 27, 30f.,
   51f., 77, 80, 89, 95, 96

Kierkegaard, Søren, 78
Kübler-Ross, Elisabeth, 5, 42f.

Lindemann, Erich, 66
Lindsay, Hal, xii, 79
Love, 33f.
Luther, Martin, 86

Man
   biblical view of, 50, 51, 87
   dualism, 83
May, Rollo, 38, 41
Medicine, 11
Miracle, 90, 93
Mitford, Jessica, 11, 12
Moltmann, Jürgen, xii

Neale, Robert, 9

Paul, St., 72f., 80
Plato, 46, 50, 84, 85
Pornography, 9
Promise, 53
Purgatory, 86

Relational theology, 19, 32, 49, 88,
   92
Relationships, 35
Resurrection
   future event, 95f.
   in present experience, 92f.
   Jesus', 54, 77, 89f.
   meaning of, 88
Rites of passage, 64

Sacrament, 64
Sartre, Jean-Paul, 53
Secularization, 2, 10, 13
Sex, 9
Sexuality, 9, 94
Sin, 68f.
Socrates, 46, 49, 84, 85
Soul, 83f.
Suffering, 19, 37

Technology, 13
Teilhard de Chardin, 31
Thielicke, Helmut, 67, 68
Tillich, Paul, 75
Toffler, Alvin, xi
Tolstoy, Leo, 61f.
Tournier, Paul, 66
Toynbee, Arnold, 1, 13

Van Gennep, Arnold, 64
Van Leeuwen, P. J., 69

Wahl, Charles, 44
Wald, George, xi
Weisman, Avery, 45
Wise, Carroll, 47
Wittgenstein, Ludwig, 57